Egypt Travel Gu

An Itinerary book about Egypt travel: The local's guide for your trip to Cairo, what to see, do and eat, tourist attractions and beyond the pyramids.

Artus Rodrigue

Table of content

EGYPT'S BEST TRADITIONAL FOOD AND RESTAURANTS

10 Arabic Phrases & Words to Improve Your Egypt Trip

Conclusion

Introduction

Egypt is the first place that comes to mind when considering the best place to spend a vacation because of its amazing history, which spans more than 4500 years, the variety of natural attractions found throughout the lovely cities of Cairo, Alexandria, Luxor, and Aswan, and don't forget about the alluring city resort of Hurghada.

First-time visitors to Egypt may have an amazing experience, but only if they are well aware of all the cultural differences, safety precautions, health concerns, and other factors that must be taken to provide the best possible trip. A lifetime spent discovering Egypt's treasures will be filled with new miracles that unveil fresh facets of creativity, ingenuity, and invention with each glance.

Egypt is a mysterious land that offers a variety of amazing sights, mouth watering cuisines, and a sense of wonder and enchantment. Travelers from throughout the globe are welcome and safe in Egypt.

This epic Egypt Itinerary travel guidebook covers all the major sites to help you make the most of your trip as you explore the land of the pharaohs. Throughout history, the mysteries of the Ancient Egyptians have served as a symbol of mystery and awe, from the recognizable Great Pyramids of Giza to astounding archeological sites like the Valley of the Kings.

The finest 10 day itineraries and best tour experiences to fully immerse yourself in the culture, scenery, and history of one of the most amazing vacation locations in the world have been compiled after spending several weeks traveling in Egypt.

Welcome to egypt

Egypt, often known as the Arab Republic of Egypt, is one of the most magnificent and fascinating nations you will ever visit. Egypt has a distinct place in its history, culture, cuisine, religion, and varied terrain for

Everyone was fortunate enough to go there.

Egypt's history is illimitable and one of the greatest legacies of human civilization, but Egypt is much more than simply its tens of thousands of year-old pyramids and other structures; Egypt is life itself, and every person can go there at least once in their lives.

What country is Egypt in?

Egypt is mostly found in the northern section of the African Continent, with a small portion of the Sinai Desert found in Asia. The distance from the very North to the very South is 1,024 kilometers, making it the 31st biggest nation in the world with a total size of 1,002,450 square kilometers.

What city in Egypt is the capital?

Egypt's capital is Cairo, pronounced Al-Qahirah, and means "the victors." Cairo, one of the largest cities on the African continent, was developed around the Nile River. Cairo is a unique metropolis with 9.5 million residents that is very diversified.

What are Egypt's major cities?

Cairo is the primary city due to its status as the nation's capital. However, other cities including Alexandria, Aswan, Luxor, Sharm El Sheik, Dahab, Gouna, and Hurghada are also important in terms of both tourism and the local economy.

What is Egypt's official currency?

The Egyptian Pound is the name of Egypt's currency. Egyptian currency is beautiful, but it has a relatively low relative worth to the English Pound, Euro, and US Dollar. EGP is an acronym for Egyptian Pounds.

Which religion predominates in Egypt?

Islam is the most common religion in Egypt, with 90% of the population being Muslims and 10% being Christians. The majority of Muslims are Sunnis, while the majority of Christians belong to the Coptic Orthodox Church.

Geographical Egypt

Egypt has coasts on both the Mediterranean and the Red Sea, and the Nile River runs through its whole length. It is strategically placed in the Gulf of Aqaba. Israel, the Gaza Strip, Sudan, and Libya are its neighbors. A little over two-thirds of Egypt's land area comprises the Western Desert. On the western side of the banks of the Nile River, there is a region of the Sahara desert called the Western Desert.

Egyptian food

Even if there are some Greek influences, such as in the north shore, Egyptian cuisine is very traditional and consists mostly of beans, lentils, pasta, rice, and bread. The cuisine Koshary, which consists of rice, lentils, pasta, tomato sauce, chickpeas, crispy onions, and garlic sauce, is well-known and traditional.

Tamiya, a bean paste-based dish, is among the best cuisines from Egypt. Another popular dish in Egypt is called molokhia, which is a soup prepared from a very nutritious, antioxidant-rich green leaf. An emblem of Egyptian food is molokhia.

Stuffed pigeons, kebabs, and kofta are some of the most popular meat and poultry dishes in Egypt. Since they have access to some of the greatest fresh seafood in the world, Egypt's cuisine also features a lot of fish and shellfish.

Arabic Arts

Art was first mentioned in Egypt during the Old Kingdom, and ever since, it has been considered to be one of the most significant facets of Egyptian culture, second only to religion.

Egypt has numerous categories, including:

Literature

Naguib Mahfouz was the first author from Egypt to be awarded the Nobel Prize for literature in the Arabic language. Muhammad Husayn Haykal, Nawa El Saadawi, Alifa Rifaat, Ahmed Fouad Negm, Salah Jaheen, and Abdel Rahman El-Abnudi are a few more well-known authors from Egypt.

Cinema

Every year, several new films are released, increasing the visibility of Egyptian cinema. Numerous series and programs are made during the Ramadan season since viewing Egyptian television series is a significant Ramadan custom. Every year, the El Gouna International Film Festival attracts talented individuals to the Egyptian and international film industries.

Music

The importance of music is enormous in Egypt, where people hold it in high regard. Umm Kulthum, Mohammed Abdel Wahab, Abdel Halim Hafez, Sayed Darwish, and Abdul al-Hamuli are a few of the legendary names in Egyptian music. Names like Amr Diab, Mohamed Mounir, Tamer Hosny, Mohamed Ramadan, and others are the new faces of Egyptian music, and contemporary music is now taking up a significant portion of the Egyptian music business.

Dance

The well-known belly dancing dance form originated in Egypt and continues to be practiced with great fervor both domestically and abroad. It is customary in Egyptian weddings to have a belly dancer join the bride and groom for their wedding reception dances.

Sport in Egypt

Sports are very popular in Egypt, and almost every café or restaurant has a television set up to watch games and tournaments.

Soccer is the most popular sport in Egypt, and despite the national team's lack of World Cup success, they have had great success in the African Cup. Because Egyptian soccer fans are so devoted to the game, they never give up hope and still hold out hope that their country will one day win the World Cup.

Egyptian squash players are among the greatest in the world, despite not being the best at soccer, and the sport, along with tennis and water polo, is very popular there.

Is Egypt safe?

Egypt is a secure destination. Although you will feel secure going alone because of the new government's tough anti-sexual harassment laws and the low crime rate, Egypt is best experienced with the assistance of a tour guide who is familiar with the region and speaks Egyptian Arabic.

What season is ideal for traveling to Egypt?

The greatest time of year to visit Egypt is between September and May when you can enjoy the outdoors of Egypt with a beautiful cool breeze and not too much heat, but enough. This is because Egypt summers can become incredibly hot, with temperatures climbing as high as 50 Celsius.

Egypt's culture

Etiquette

In Egypt, modesty in behavior and attire is highly regarded. A certain kind of dress code, which mandates attire that covers the whole body save the hands and face, has an impact on women more than males.

Although there are numerous additional designs, from merely covering the hair to covering the full face, for women, this is most obviously accomplished by donning a headscarf that covers the hair and ears and is fastened under the chin. This is the sense in which veiling is practiced in Egypt, yet the environment is unstable and quite diverse. Many ladies don't wear any kind of veil at all. In today's Egypt, there is a lot of discussion over what is appropriate, essential, or obligatory. There are several reasons why women choose to cover themselves, from those who believe it is an

obligation under Islam to others who do so just to appease their male and female relatives. Men are also urged to dress modestly, but the modifications are less pronounced and include things like loose pants and long sleeves. The idea behind this is that clothing should cover up the form of the body for both men and women.

Another etiquette guideline is that introductions must come before any kind of social contact. Any new member of a group, even one made up of strangers, is required to introduce themselves to the existing members. In less private settings, handshakes are appropriate. Another typical welcome gesture is to embrace someone, generally someone of the same sex.

In general, people are addressed by their first name, frequently followed by a title of some sort ('am, or uncle, is the all-purpose title for men; other options include hajj for a pilgrim returned from Mecca or simply for an older man, duktor for a person with a doctorate, and muhandis for an engineer). It is rude to address someone just by name.

Treating visitors with courtesy and hospitality is one of the most fundamental etiquette rules. The very minimum a guest may hope for is an offering, often tea or a soft drink. It's common to refer to the first beverage as a "greeting." Cigarettes are often provided as a form of hospitality. Some individuals in rural places avoid going to persons they see as of lower status than themselves. The higher-status host extends hospitality to the lower-status visitor, therefore from this perspective, visits are always "up" and hospitality is always "down."

In general, young people respect older people and women and men. Younger people are required to treat their elders with respect, refrain from making fun of them, and use particular forms of address for grandparents, aunts, uncles, and other elderly nonrelatives. Juniors should refrain from speaking loudly to seniors and from staying sitting while an elder gets up. There is an increase in respectful forms of address due to growing class gaps and the growth of patronage links. This includes the return of designations like Pasha and Bey which were formerly recognized titles but were banned after 1952.

Religion

Beliefs in religion. A nation of "everyday piety" is Egypt. The oneness of God, whose truths were revealed through the prophet Muhammad, is the fundamental principle of Islam. One of the five foundations of religion is the declaration of this

fundamental confession of faith. The other four are the five daily prayers, the pilgrimage to Mecca, the Ramadan fast, and almsgiving. These five pillars summarize Muslim thought and practice for many people. Egyptians commonly refer to God and his majesty. Any proclamation regarding the future, for instance, is likely to end with the phrase "God willing," signifying that God alone has the last say in whether or not to carry out the goal.

There are further potential elaborations in Egypt. Some people who place a strong emphasis on the all-powerfulness of God engage in religious practice by praying for guidance in resolving issues and hoping for beneficial results, such as healing from illness or bad luck. Several customs involving pilgrimages to shrines have developed around this idea, including

- Artifacts from pharaohs' tombs are shown at the Egyptian Museum in Cairo.

- Artifacts from pharaohs' tombs are shown at the Egyptian Museum in Cairo.

to seek the intercession of those who are buried there and who are said to be beloved by God. The most important of these shrines are those in Cairo connected to the Prophet Muhammad's family. However, there are similar shrines in every town and hamlet, varying in significance. Religious purists often criticize this kind of religion, claiming that placing such a high value on these "saints" undermines the concept of the unity of God.

Associations of mystics are also quite widespread in Egypt (Sufi brotherhoods). These male-dominated organizations are led by a shaykh or a hierarchy of shaykhs who are committed to assisting their followers in experiencing a mystical union with God. The group rites known as zikr, which are exclusive to each order, are often used to achieve this mystical experience. There are about six million members in the roughly 100 officially recognized organizations as well as many more that are not (about one-third of the adult male population).

Focusing on Islamic fundamentalism and being knowledgeable about Islamic "law," or the specific rules of conduct that devout Muslims must follow to live under God's will as understood by experts is the currently dominant practice in Egypt. The Koran, which is God's word, is the source of authority in this case. Imams, who conduct the prayers, maybe anybody who is in good standing with their religion, however, established mosques often have a permanent imam. A khatib, many of whom have training in religious institutions, delivers the sermon on Friday. There have been discussions over whether women can fill these positions, particularly the one of a religious instructor for women and girls.

The Grand Mufti, who provides authorized interpretations of the Koran, and the Shaykh al-Azhar, who oversees the religious bureaucracy, are the two most important religious figures in Egyptian Islam. It is well known that the people holding these positions have differing opinions on some topics.

The feast that follows the fasting month of Ramadan and 'Id al-Adha, which coincides with the Muslim pilgrimage to Mecca, are the two greatest holy occasions for Muslims. After a month of fasting and family visits, the Ramadan vacation is when people often simply relax. Most families attempt to sacrifice a ram on this day in observance of Abraham's readiness to sacrifice his son, who was miraculously transformed into a ram. Other religious festivals include the Islamic New Year, which is observed on the first day of the month of Moharram, and Moulid an-Nabi, which commemorates the birth of the prophet Muhammad and is particularly significant to sufis.

As the day of the weekly congregational prayer in Islam, Friday signifies the end of the workweek without officially being a "day of rest." The two-day weekend is Friday and Saturday in modern Egypt. Thus, Sunday through Thursday is the typical work and school week, however, some people additionally work on Saturday. On this timetable, Christians go to church in the evenings and save Friday for significant celebrations.

The Coptic Orthodox Church is a branch of the early Christian Patriarchate of Alexandria's affiliated churches. It serves as Egypt's primary Christian church. Its monophysite theology maintains that there is just one nature, both human and divine, in Jesus Christ. A patriarch serves as the leader of the Coptic church, which is also assisted by bishops and parish priests. The Coptic church places a strong emphasis on monasticism, and the patriarch is chosen from the ranks of monks rather than priests.

When a patriarch passes away, his successor is chosen by lot (i.e., by God) from a select group of contenders who have made it through the selection procedure. For Copts, the monasteries serve as places of worship and retreats. The Virgin Mary is currently honored, and several churches are devoted

to her.

The Christmas and Easter seasons are the two primary Christian festivals. Minor festivals include those that are extensions of these seasons, such as "Id al-Ghattas" (Epiphany), "Christ's Baptism," "Palm Sunday," and several connected to the Virgin Mary (Ascension, in mid-August, is the main one).

Egyptian Muslims and Christians are alike in the majority of areas of life apart from religion. Both share daily devotional practices and many fundamental religious principles. The careful observer may sometimes see distinguishing characteristics, such as Muslim women's "Islamic" attire or a cross on the inside of the right wrist on Christians. Names are also often, though not always, telling. Most of the time, the difference is meaningless to most individuals. However, sometimes there are those on either side who emphasize the differences and accuse the other of discrimination or unfairness.

Rarely do such statements result in more aggressive behavior. However, the line is maintained, and both groups either discourage or forbid marriages and conversion. Residential segregation between Muslims and Christians does not exist; instead, Christian communities are scatted among Muslim neighborhoods. In contemporary times, the coexistence of Muslims and Christians has hampered efforts to characterize Egypt as a Muslim nation, favoring secularism at least indirectly.

Rituals and sacred locations.

Another significant element of religious activity is the ritualization of life's phases, which is generally shared by Muslims and Christians. One week after a baby is born, Egyptians celebrate a naming ceremony that combines Islamic (or Coptic) and "traditional" features and serves primarily as a family celebration to welcome the new member into the family.

All males are circumcised, often as neonates, and before puberty, most girls are also "circumcised". (Although female genital mutilation takes many different forms, polls indicate that both Christians and Muslims in Egypt, as well as around 97 percent of girls overall, are afflicted.) Egyptian society places a lot of emphasis on marriage. Muslims see it as a contract, the signing of which is then followed by a family celebration; Christians view it as a sacrament, which often takes place in a church and is followed by a family celebration the same day.

Death and life after death.

Both Muslims and Christians attempt to bury the dead the same day after death. We send our condolences right away, again in 40 days, and again in a year. Readings from the Koran are often used to commemorate Islamic condolence gatherings. The soul is seen as distinct from other noncorporeal elements of the person, such as the double, the brother/sister, and the ghost, by both Muslims and Christians. While some of the other elements vanish with death or only manifest after death, the "soul" endures both before and after birth.

Economy and Food

Food in Everyday Life Eating is a significant social activity that is essential to celebrating ceremonial occasions and special occasions.The bread loaf is the most significant food item in everyday life. In rural regions, women often make bread at home in mud ovens. Bakeries sell bread in urban areas. The government closely controls the weight and dimensions of the standard loaf.

It is one of the very few goods that still get a governmental subsidy and is reasonably priced.

The native diet makes extensive use of legumes. Foul is a prominent national dish. Fava beans are cooked in this recipe gently over low heat while being seasoned with salt, lemon, cumin, and oil. Breakfast is often when it's consumed. Tamiya or falafel, which is prepared with mashed fava beans combined with onions and leeks and cooked in oil, is another popular meal. Another well-liked dish is koshari, a combination of rice, black lentils, and macaroni topped with tomato sauce and fried onions. These foods are made at home but are also offered for sale at booths across Cairo.

The amount of animal protein consumed is largely influenced by economic status (and is itself a sign of wealth). Rich families regularly consume animal protein (beef, lamb, chicken, or fish). Pork is not eaten by Muslims. Families with lower incomes consume animal protein once or even twice each month.

All around the nation, there are many restaurants. They range from upscale eateries providing foreign cuisine to food stands selling traditional street food.

The setting and meal service are two key differences between traditional, mostly rural, and urban middle-class dining customs. In villages, people eat at low circular wooden tables while sitting on carpets. Everyone eats straight from the serving dish with a spoon provided for each individual. Around Western-style dining tables, people sit on chairs in urban settings. Everybody has their plate, fork, spoon, and knife. The main meal is often eaten after midnight in rural regions and the late afternoon when office employees return to their homes in urban areas.

Food Traditions during Festive Occasions. Special dinners are served to commemorate certain Muslim feasts. Those who can afford to sacrifice a ram must do so on 'Eid al-Adha, which commemorates Abraham's readiness to offer up his son (who was then miraculously transformed into a ram). The household's members and the needy each get a portion of the animal.

To commemorate the end of the Ramadan fast, special cookies (kahk) are baked and then dusted with powdered sugar. Typically, visitors who carry the feast's greetings are

given these biscuits.

Halawet al-mulid, a variety of sweets prepared with various nuts, is consumed to commemorate the Prophet's Birthday, which commemorates the birth of the prophet Muhammad. Boys or girls get horses or dolls that are constructed of sugar and painted with colorful paper.

Orthodox Copts break their fast with a variety of meals composed of beef and fowl on the night of both Christmas and Easter. Similar to the cookies made for 'Id al-Fitr, cookies are one of the key foods that commemorate the feast. Easter Monday is primarily recognized by a salt-fish, spring onion, lettuce, and colorful egg meal that is served outside in gardens and open spaces. Almost every area in the country participates in this event, and people from all socioeconomic strata attend. It is the spring and harvest celebration of ancient Egypt.

Both Muslims and Christians see fasting as a spiritual practice. Muslims must refrain from eating and drinking from dawn until sunset, especially during the lunar month of Ramadan (either twenty-nine or thirty days). Other Islamic holidays, such as those honoring the prophet Muhammad's birth or his miraculous "Night Journey," the days that mark the middle of the lunar month (days thirteen, fourteen, and fifteen), or every Monday and Thursday, are also observed by certain exceptionally pious Muslims as fast days. As a consequence, some people might regard over half of the days in a year to be fasting days. Almost all Muslims in Egypt fast throughout Ramadan, whereas fewer people observe the optional fasts.

Even more, days are potentially permissible for fasting for Egyptian Christians. The number varies, but it includes more than 200 days annually, mostly around Christmas and Easter as well as every Wednesday and Friday that fall outside of the fasting times. Avoiding meat, fish, eggs, milk, butter, and cheese is the definition of a Christian fast. The mind's dominance over the body and emotions to achieve greater purity is one of the themes of fasting in the Christian faith.

Simple Economy. Agriculture accounts for around 18% of the gross domestic output, while industry contributes 25%. All other activities, largely services, including tourism, and the "informal sector" make up the remaining 57%. (small-scale enterprises that often escape government supervision). A sizable building sector and a vast network of banks are also present. The 1990s saw the emergence of a stock market where roughly thirty companies are traded.

Egypt has some of the best yields per acre in the whole globe, making it a wealthy agricultural nation. The principal crops are cotton, sugarcane, wheat, maize, and fava beans; sizable portions are also dedicated to vegetable and fruit plantations, mainly citrus. Cattle, water buffalo, sheep, and goats are examples of major livestock, and some land is utilized to cultivate crops for their sustenance. On average, there are two crops per year. While some farmers, like those who cultivate wheat, aim to be self-sufficient, on the whole, they sell what they raise and buy their food from the market.

Small-scale merchants buy food crops through elaborate market networks and trade them into metropolitan regions or sometimes between rural areas. Overall, the marketing industry is made up of a lot of small businesses, however, a few large-scale trade firms are active. Farmers must accept the trader's offer since they are too tiny to negotiate a better price.

Land, water, and labor are agriculture's three primary inputs. Private persons often own tiny parcels of land, with an average size of roughly 2.5 acres (1 hectare). Tenancies were guaranteed from 1952 to 1997 (people renting farms could not be kicked out unless in very exceptional circumstances), but this assurance was removed in 1997. By that time, around one-sixth of the property was under rent, and renters tended to be less wealthy than farmers who were also owners. However, renters had become used to treating fields as if they were their own, and after 1997, they had to accept either an increase in rent or the loss of the land.

Egyptian agriculture relies heavily on irrigation, and the government provides water to the farmer via a system of canals. Water is reimbursed indirectly via the bigger farmers' land taxes. Water is seen as being free, and the government still supports the idea that farmers should get free water. Farmers do pay a price for having to move the water from the canals to their crops.

Based on the rural family home, farm work is generally done by family members. The leader of this home mobilizes labor from his family but may also sometimes recruit outside labor, especially for jobs that call for a large group to cooperate. Egyptian agriculture is often labor-intensive, therefore gardening would be a better comparison.

Likely, many of these rural homes would not exist without the revenue from the job performed by the numerous members who work as agricultural workers or in industries unrelated to agriculture. Government employment (as teachers, clerks, or guards), independent enterprise (as in selling or shipping agricultural products), and industrial labor are the most typical non-farm sources of income.

The parts of Egyptian agriculture that can be automated, such as plowing, carrying, or using a water pump, are called agriculture. Planting, weeding, and harvesting are a few more duties that are still carried out by hand. Most farmers rent equipment as they need it since they cannot afford to buy it. In general, wealthier farmers possess tractors and pumps and rent out their extra capacity.

Principal Industries. Egypt is a moderately industrialized nation, particularly in the production of weaponry, cement, textiles, and clothing. Egypt is home to many vehicle manufacturers' assembly lines. Many of these industries were held by the government in the second part of the 20th century. They were being privatized around the turn of the twenty-first century. The production of shoes, door frames, furniture, apparel, metal pots, and similar things for local use also takes place in several small, private workshops.

Trade. More often than not, Egypt imports more than it exports. Consumer items, including food, and raw materials for the industry are included in imports; agricultural products and services make up the majority of exports. The export of Egyptian laborers who work abroad and bring money home is a significant one.

What to know before traveling to Egypt

Here are a few key travel guidelines you should be aware of before you go to Cairo for the trip of a lifetime.

EGYPTIAN VISAS

Egypt requires a visa for those arriving by air. Fortunately, visitors from many nations, including those from the US, UK, Australia, Europe, and many regions of Asia, may get a visa on arrival. When you arrive at Cairo International Airport, you may acquire this for USD 25 at the bank stand. Strangely, you must pay for this in cash in either US dollars or Egyptian pounds (EGP).

A word of advice: visitors from a few nations, such as Indonesia and the Philippines, will need a valid visa from your country's embassy or consulate. Before you

go, make sure to review the most recent

rules.

FOR THIS EGYPT ITINERARY, INSURANCE

It's reasonable to state that travel insurance is now essentially required in light of the recent incidents.

I endorse SafetyWing and World Nomads as two insurance providers.

World Nomads is a fantastic choice for quick journeys, particularly for adventurers. You cannot top SafetyWing's offering if you're considering a much longer stay or if you're a digital nomad (this is what I use).

APARTMENTS IN EGYPT

I'll highlight some of the top hotels in Giza, Cairo, Luxor, and Aswan throughout this tour. These will be based on my own experiences staying at these hotels and provide some of the top choices for different price ranges.

Otherwise, Booking.com is the finest website for lodging reservations in Egypt.

Note: When making hotel reservations, be careful to read the small print about the city/tourist tax. Even though it's unimportant, it's often not seen on the first page.

INTERNAL TRANSPORT IN EGYPT

In this Egypt itinerary, I suggest using overnight trains to cover the huge distances (sleeper trains).

The fact that you won't lose any valuable days in transit makes them surprisingly pleasant and, in my view, the greatest method of transportation inside Egypt.

Another option is to take a flight between places like Cairo and Aswan. However, the cost is often higher. Egypt Air is unquestionably the greatest airline, and they even provide meals and luggage up to 23 KG for every journey, if you demand (for domestic and international flights). For comparing prices, I advise using Skyscanner. I advise utilizing Uber when available (now just in Cairo) for local transportation inside cities, and taxis in other locations.

Buses are another excellent low-cost alternative, with several lines operating between major cities. A dependable website is GoBus.

Tourists often use the Nile Cruise to go from Aswan to Luxor. The majority of the sights on this itinerary will often be seen on these visits as well. At the bottom of this piece, I've included some recommendations for the Nile Cruise option.

INFORMATION ON EGYPTIAN TIPPING CULTURE

Before you even leave the airport, you could notice that Egyptians will attempt to obtain a tip from you for nearly everything.
You'll hear the phrase baksheesh used virtually daily.

Don't be duped into giving tips for blatantly absurd things. Tipping is customary for services like cabs, restaurants, tour guides, and even a selfie (which you'll be asked for). For instance, I was ready to go through security screening when a guy surged in front of me, grabbed my bag, and flung it through. I was then asked for a gratuity.

Egyptian travel advice

At the Cairo airport, how can I acquire a SIM card?

Obtaining a local SIM card is another action you should do after landing in Egypt. Three mobile phone carriers' booths can be seen on your left as you exit the arrivals area of the building: Vodafone, Etisalat, and Orange. Only since Orange had the smallest queue at the time, I obtained my card there.

I simply wanted internet data, therefore I purchased 3,5GB of it for 100 EGP. The whole process was simple and just took a few minutes. To get the card, all I required was my passport; the installation and operation of the card were handled by others. I can't complain about the coverage since it was generally functional everywhere I went. Only sometimes did the signal on the train go out. I was pleased with the internet speed and can suggest obtaining an Orange card.

Shopping And Money

The official currency of Egypt is the Egyptian Pound, however, all hotels, restaurants, and ATMs also take US and European dollars and euros. Tipping is a significant aspect of Egyptian society as well; a common sum is 5 or 10 pounds, and a 10% tip at restaurants is well-known all across the city. Every tourist should haggle for the greatest deal while purchasing.

Get the Right Packaging

Everyone should make sure they have everything they need to be packed before departing for Egypt, including any prescription medications, water bottles, toilet paper, credit or debit cards, and any other important goods. Every tourist should include all the necessities, including a universal adapter, a VPN connection, a power bank, glasses, a hat, a scarf, sunblock, comfortable shoes, light, soft clothing, and more, to enjoy their trip to the fullest.

Everybody from across the globe is always welcome to enter Egypt via its borders. The heavenly historical and ecological wonders of these sacred regions may provide travelers with the trip of a lifetime. If you don't know how to prepare for a trip then check out this page

Know Your Environment

Before visiting Egypt, every visitor should learn about the country's culture. Although Egypt's culture is liberal, it is nevertheless highly traditional, so be careful to dress modestly. To converse with the general populace, it is also advisable to know a few Arabic terms.

Transportation in Egypt

Have you ever wondered how Egyptians get about their crowded cities?
Not on camels, please!
In Egypt, three different modes of transportation link towns together: land, sea, and air.

Since Cairo is Egypt's capital, it is where they are most concentrated.

With a variety of modes of transportation, including the metro, bus, river bus, etc., you may go from one location to another with ease. Some of these modes of transportation, like the River Bus and Nile Taxi, are more practical and entertaining for visitors.

Let's learn more!

Transportation on Land

Several highways connect Egypt to both Africa and Asia. A growing network of roads, including the Ring Road, Alexandria Desert Road, and Geish Road, links Cairo to neighboring cities. Roadways in Egypt often have various benefits, including well-metaled ways and flexible, flat terrain. In Egypt, there are a variety of options to travel by road, including:

Metro

Cairo has a comprehensive metro system that serves numerous districts. It has three lines and stops at 92 stations across the city. Compared to the first and second lines, the third one is more refined and cozy. Soon, the fourth line will open.

Railways

The Middle East and Africa's oldest railroad system is the Egyptian railway system. Because shorter trips are often slower and less pleasant, it is preferable for longer trips rather than shorter ones like Cairo to Alexandria travel. The train has three different carriage classes; the first and second ones may have air conditioning. Sleeping trains and air-conditioned trains are available, however, the cost will be much more than for regular trains. The mainline train schedule is readily available since it is released every six months. In Egypt, trains are regarded as a secure mode of transportation.

Buses

In Egypt, buses are among the most often used forms of transportation. In addition to a vast number of governorates including Alexandria, Port Said, Ismailia, Sharm El Sheikh, and North and South Sinai, they are extensively dispersed in Cairo and Giza. The bus is not the most efficient way to go because of its slowness from stopping at several stops, the intense traffic, and the challenge of getting a seat during rush hour. However, it is accessible and regarded as one of the least expensive forms of transportation. Take a ticket after you pay the fare so you may subsequently confirm your payment. Each bus has a distinct line and a distinct number inscribed in Arabic on the front at the top region of the driver.

Microbuses

Microbuses are renowned for moving at a rapid pace. Additionally, they are particularly common in Cairo and all other governorates. They are smaller than buses, you must seat since there is nowhere to stand, which makes microbuses a better mode of transportation than buses, the fee varies depending on the distance traveled, and there is no ticket. Since you can discover microbuses at certain stations and stop them on the road, they are simple to operate.

Taxis

In Egypt, taxis are among the most popular modes of transportation since they are quicker and more laid-back. However, they are more costly than other options, and you risk being tricked by the fee sometimes, therefore it is preferable to urge the driver to use the meter or negotiate the fare with him. Although there are no taxi stands, you may stop any cab that is driving by. It is important to note here the availability of Uber and Careem, two private automobile services that can be booked using a special app from your mobile shop. They are superior to a regular taxi since the fare is determined using a certain method, and you know it before you get in the car. Their autos are also quicker and more practical. Because the drivers utilize GPS to determine the best and quickest route, you'll never get lost with them.

A tuk-tuk

One of the newest modes of transportation in Egypt is the tuk-tuk. They are widespread in cities and small towns, and they may be

found in many governorates and regions. Tuk Tuks have benefits, such as affordable fares and the ease with which they can navigate congested and tiny streets. It also has drawbacks; for example, it is seen as risky and only travels inside the confines of tiny regions rather than taking you to well-known locations.

Transportation via Water

Bus River

One of the earliest modes of transportation in contemporary Egypt is the river bus. You may use the river bus if your destination is located along the river. It will keep you out of the gridlock, but it moves more slowly than other modes of transportation.

Transportation by air

Airplanes

The best mode of transportation in Egypt to go from Cairo to other governorates like Sharm el-Sheik is via flight. Although it is the most costly, quickest, and most comfortable mode of transportation. This service is provided by a local business in Egypt, called Egypt Air.

Tourists' transportation

When visiting Egypt, visitors should choose a mode of transportation that will allow them to view the country's famous attractions. For instance, they may take the river bus, which will take them to Old Cairo's famous Coptic neighborhood. The view of the Nile makes it a lovely mode of transportation. Additionally, various modes of transportation are useful for visitors, such as:

In Nile Taxis

The Nile taxi is another option for those who want to see the Nile and save time. Compared to the river bus, they are faster. There are two kinds of Nile taxis: those that you must wait for until enough people have boarded, and those that you may reserve in advance at a convenient time for you.

Carriages

Travelers may explore distant cities and view provincial cities by using carriages as a mode of transportation. They frequently can go where the cab cannot, notwithstanding their delay. The majority of its usage nowadays is for sightseeing, particularly on vacations and special events. The Nile Corniche, Downtown, Zamalek, and Giza are the primary locations where carriages may be found.

Autonomous Vehicles

For visitors, it is a practical mode of transportation. The motorist must possess an international driving permit. It may be rented from hotels or travel businesses. The kind of vehicle determines the fare.

Both locals and visitors may navigate Egypt using a variety of public and private modes of transportation. You have a choice of modes of transportation, including land, water, and air. There are affordable transportation options including buses and metros. Taxis and microbuses are two speedier transportation options. Additionally, you may find Tuk Tuks in lanes, villages, and many other locations; they can go along small paths inside certain bounds. Whether you are an Egyptian or visiting Egypt, you shouldn't miss taking the River bus to Old Cairo to take in the peace. Take carriages for touring if you wish to view far-off cities. If you want to travel comfortably, board an aircraft.

EGYPT ITINERARIES FOR TEN DAYS

THE ULTIMATE ITINERARY FOR EGYPT IN 10 DAYS

DAY 1: GET TO CAIRO

I won't lie; arriving in Cairo, the capital of Egypt may seem a bit chaotic.

Once you enter Cairo, the sixth-most populated city in the world, you'll immediately notice it. As a result, I've set aside this first day to recuperate before beginning my somewhat brisk journey across Egypt.

There are other day excursions you may do from Cairo, however, if you arrive early. A trip to Alexandria, which has attractions like the Bibliotheca Alexandrina and the Catacombs of Kom el-Shoqafa, is among the most well-liked. A Nile dinner cruise or

Cairo trips to the Bahariya Desert are other alternatives (White Desert).

A PLACE TO RESIDE IN GIZA

I strongly suggest spending the first night in Giza. The Great Pyramids on the Giza Plateau and the neighboring Saqqara Necropolis are the first stops on this epic Egyptian itinerary's second day, which explains why.

Here are my top three suggestions for places to stay in Giza.

Marriott Mena House - With views of the Great Pyramids of Giza from its opulent air-conditioned suites, this five-star hotel

features 40 acres of magnificent gardens.

The Great Pyramid Inn is the hotel with the greatest views of the pyramids for the money. Every morning, a breakfast buffet is offered, which you may savor while taking in the dawn over the historic sites.

The Great Sphinx is within a short 4-minute walk from the Comfort Pyramids Inn, which should delight everybody. For those on a budget who wish to enjoy a 5-star view of the Great Pyramids, this hotel is fantastic.

MORE ON BOOKING.COM

DAY 2: GIZA, SAQQARA, and CAIRO

On this spectacular Egypt travel path, day two is often the day you've been looking forward to.
You will get the opportunity to see the enormous Giza Pyramids, the mysterious Saqqara Necropolis, and the Sphinx. As there is so much to understand, I strongly suggest obtaining an Egyptologist tour of these places.

NECROPOLIS SAQQARA

The earliest Egyptian pyramid, the Pyramid of Djoser, also known as the Step Pyramid, is located in the Saqqara Necropolis, which

is the first stop on the tour.

This was built more than 100 years before the Great Pyramid, between 2667 and 2648 BCE. This is a fantastic location to study Old Kingdom Egyptian history and tour the ancient temples, mastaba, pyramids, and tombs in the Memphis Necropolis.

THE MAJOR GIZA PYRAMIDS

The Great Pyramids of Giza are without a doubt the most spectacular buildings ever built. Exploring these ancient treasures

might take hours.

The Great Pyramid (Khufu Pyramid), the Pyramid of Khafre, and the Pyramid of Menkaure are the three principal pyramids on the Giza Plateau (along with the three adjacent Queen Pyramids).

Many people would consider the Great Pyramids of Giza to be the highlight of their

10-day trip to Egypt, even though there are many more sites that will astound you. Enjoy this time!

Advice: If you can stand the heat, I strongly suggest spending the extra 400 EGP to enter the Great Pyramid. This is an opportunity you shouldn't miss.

THE GIZA GREAT SPHINX

The famous Great Sphinx is Giza's last sight

to see.

It should go without saying that the Sphinx, which is not far from the Great Pyramids, is an unquestionable must-see for everyone visiting Egypt!

You may be surprised to learn that the Sphinx has a separate temple complex outside of this incredible rock. In actuality, the Sphinx-carving bedrock was used by the ancient Egyptians to chisel enormous limestone stones for this temple.

FLY OR TAKE A SLEEPER TRAIN TO ASWAN

The first leg of this 10-day itinerary's transportation comprises a 900-kilometer (560-mile) trip from Cairo to Aswan, leaving Lower Egypt behind (for now).

As I indicated previously, the overnight train is the ideal option to preserve important exploration time since you have your cabin, and is surprisingly comfy. Depending on the timetable, the trip from

Cairo to Aswan might take anywhere between 9 and 12 hours.

However, because Egyptian trains aren't quite on time, it's a good idea to arrive at the

railway station early.

Flying straight to Aswan is an additional alternative. EgyptAir is my top pick since their regular tickets include luggage.

PHILAE TEMPLE & UNFINISHED OBELISK IN ASWAN ON DAY 3

Leave your belongings at your lodging when you wake up since day three is another full day of seeing historic sites! Aswan offers a wide variety of activities, and this schedule includes most of the top highlights and sights.

OBELISK UNFINISHED

In a former granite quarry site not far from the city of Aswan, there lies a massive 1,000-ton granite structure known as The

Unfinished Obelisk. This enormous obelisk would have been the tallest and heaviest structure in the world even though it was never finished. Today, it gives tourists a glimpse into the process used to chisel out these massive limestone pillars by the ancient Egyptians.

Philippine Temple

The majestic Philae Temple, which is home to the god's Isis, Osiris, and Horus, is the next stop on the tour. Despite being a very old location, the bulk of this temple was erected about 280 BCE, during the Ptolemaic dynasty and under the rule of Ptolemy II. It's incredible to think that this temple was built 2000 years after the Great Pyramids!

You must take a little boat ride to reach Agilika Island, where Philae Temple is located. From its enormous columned halls

to its many smaller temples devoted to

different deities, there is plenty to see here.

Did you know: A group of engineers and archaeologists disassembled Abu Simbel, the Philae Temple, and other magnificent structures piece by piece before moving them to other locations? This was a result of the massive Aswan High Dam project, which put them in danger of harm from the rising Nile.

LOCATIONS IN ASWAN

As opposed to Luxor or Cairo, Aswan doesn't provide as many lodging possibilities. Even yet, there are still some excellent hotels to be found here. My top three options are listed below.

The Sofitel Legend Old Cataract provides fantastic views and 5-star service and is situated in the Nubian Desert, 1.3 kilometers from the heart of Aswan. The accommodations include an indoor and outdoor pool, a spa, and exercise facilities. The rooms are exquisitely constructed and furnished.

The Tulip Aswan Hotel is the ideal option for travelers on a budget who wish to enjoy 5-star elegance with a view of the Nile River. You may find a breakfast buffet, poolside bar service, and well-furnished air-conditioned rooms here.

The Mango Guest House is a guesthouse that is only a quick water taxi ride away from Aswan's well-known monuments. It is situated on a tiny island in the Nile River. It is within a five-minute walk from the Nile and provides everything you need at a reasonable price.

MORE ON BOOKING.COM

ASWAN to ABU SIMBEL on Day 4

The amazing Abu Simbel Temples are a pair of temples that are situated 173 miles (280 kilometers) south of Aswan.

To travel this far only to view one historic landmark is not reasonable. But let me assure you that a visit to Abu Simbel is well worthwhile! Some claim that you didn't experience Ancient Egypt if you didn't see Abu Simbel. I usually agree with them!

DAY TRIP TO ABU SIMBEL

Two enormous rock-cut temples built into the slope are known as the Abu Simbel Temples. Ramesses II, often known as Ramesses The Great, is honored with the dedication of the Great Temple. He ruled the New Kingdom for more than 66 years, at what many believe to be the apex of Ancient Egyptian civilization, making him probably the most famous Egyptian Pharaoh.

The whole temple, both inside and out, is carved from a single block of granite. The enormous colossi of Ramesses II and the Hypostyle Hall, which has six enormous sculptures of Osiris and various side rooms to explore, are among the site's highlights.

DAY 5: SAILING WITH FELUCCA (NILE RIVER)

One of my favorite experiences from my trip to Egypt occurs on the fifth day of my itinerary.

One of the world's oldest still-existing sailing vessel designs is the felucca, which was created by the Ancient Egyptians. The first societies to achieve significant advancements in shipbuilding were the Egyptians. Many people think that this is where wind-powered maritime navigation began for humans. One of the most exciting and delightful experiences in Upper Egypt is spending two days sailing and sleeping on the River Nile. It is a well-deserved vacation from touring historical monuments.

Optional: You might alter your itinerary to include an additional night in Aswan. On land, there is a lot to see, including:

The Nubian Museum

The Qubbet El-Hawa

Church of St. Simien

Agatha Christie wrote Death on the Nile at The Old Cataract Hotel.

FELUCCA SAILING ON DAY 6 (NILE

RIVER)

My view is that a two-day felucca sailing excursion is the ideal length of time. Elephantine Island and, if you're fortunate, a Nubian village are frequent stops. A better experience than a Nile Cruise is this one!

DAY 7: ON THE WAY TO LUXOR; EDU TEMPLE AND KOM OMBO TEMPLE

Now that we've had two fantastic days on the Nile, it's time to start traveling north. There is still much to see, including many of the greatest ancient attractions, so don't worry!

This 10-day itinerary for Egypt includes an overland trip from Aswan to Luxor on day seven. The Edfu Temple (Temple of Horus) and the Kom Ombo Temple are two must-see sites along the route. Being on a tour is advantageous for seeing these specific sites since there isn't much in the way of public transportation to get to these attractions.

It's preferable to remain in Luxor, which will serve as your headquarters for the last few days of your trip across Upper Egypt, after seeing the attractions.

THE CROCODILE MUMMY MUSEUM & KOM OMBO TEMPLE

One of Egypt's most distinctive temples, Kom Ombo Temple, needs to unquestionably be on your schedule if you're traveling between Luxor and Aswan.

This location is characterized as a "double" temple, divided to worship the falcon deity Haroeris and the crocodile god Sobek (Horus the Elder). The most notable sight here, despite the splendor of the temples, courts, and halls, is the ancient Egyptian calendar carved into one of the walls.

Visitors may also visit a recently opened crocodile mummy exhibit at the foot of the temple.

Temple Edfu (TEMPLE OF HORUS)

Another magnificent Ptolemaic temple, the Edfu Temple, honors Horus, the falcon, one of the most significant gods of ancient Egypt.

The whole temple complex is stunning and well-maintained. There is a sizable courtyard as well as a lovely room with columns that are filled with wonderful sculptures and hieroglyphs.

LODGING OPTIONS IN LUXOR

Due to the abundance of temples and historical landmarks, Luxor, the former capital of Thebes, is known as "The City of a Thousand Gates." On the east bank of the Nile lies the majority of the attractions, including the Luxor Temple and the Karnak Temple.

So staying on this side makes the most sense. Here are some of the best choices for accommodations in Luxor for different price ranges.

The Hilton Luxor Resort & Spa is tucked away on the banks of the Nile River and provides luxurious accommodations, a spa, and a total of seven bars. The pinnacle of

luxury resorts may be found in Upper Egypt.

The Steigenberger Nile Palace is a luxurious hotel with spacious, elegantly appointed interiors situated in the center of Luxor. The buffet is among the nicest I've ever eaten, and the prices for the luxurious accommodations are extremely low.

The greatest choice for travelers on a tight budget is the Sweet Hostel in Luxor. Every morning, a complimentary la carte breakfast is provided for guests, and the area is a wonderful starting point for seeing Luxor's famous attractions, including the Luxor Temple, which is only a 9-minute walk away!

MORE ON BOOKING.COM

LUXOR - EAST BANK ITINERARY FOR DAY 8

The eighth day of your journey across Egypt will bring you to Luxor, the Theban capital of ancient Egypt.

Due to the contemporary city's location on the Nile, it is preferable to divide an agenda for Luxor into two days of exploration of the east and west banks.

TEMPLE KARNAK

The biggest and one of the most revered temple complexes in the whole world is the Karnak Temple. It has been continuously built since at least 2,000 BCE, and its entire land area is about 250,000 square meters

(2.69 million square feet).

I strongly advise spending at least a few hours at this incredible historic location since you may easily get lost there. The enormous columns are out of this world, with incredible carvings and bright decorations.

The Karnak obelisks of Hatshepsut, which stand 28 meters tall and were carved from a single 343-ton chunk of pink granite, are the highest obelisks in Egypt still standing.

The Luxor Temple

The Luxor Temple is the next stop. Another amazing temple built about 1400 BCE is this one. According to Egyptologists, the ancients utilized this location to enthrone new Pharaohs. It was thus among the most important sacred sites in ancient Thebes.
Although smaller than Karnak Temple, the Luxor Temple is unquestionably a highlight of our east bank trip. Since this temple has some of the greatest lighting in the nation, I strongly suggest going at night or in the late afternoon.

LUXOR - WEST BANK ITINERARY FOR DAY 9

The far-off country to the west is referred to as the Duat in Egyptian mythology. For the sun to rise each morning and bring life back to earth, the solar god Ra must journey here every night to fight App.

Additionally, the Duat is where afterlife judgment takes place for souls. Because of this, the ancient Egyptians created their cemeteries in the region west of the Nile.
It's time to reveal the west bank itinerary of Luxor, where you'll find the one and only Valley of the Kings, after nine days in Egypt.

Optional: Luxor is among the top locations for hot air ballooning on the planet. Every morning, popular (and very reasonably priced) dawn excursions leave from the west bank, giving you a breathtaking view of the Valley of the Kings and the sun rising over the Nile River.

THE KINGS' VALLEY

Ancient Thebes' royal necropolis is known as the Valley of the Kings. 63 royal tombs have been found here in total by archaeologists. Each cave-like tomb is hewn out of the rock, and many include dazzlingly ornamented tunnels, halls, and burial

chambers.

Any traveler's list of things to do in Egypt must include exploring the Valley of the Kings. Approximately eleven tombs are now accessible to the public. The young king Tutankhamun, whose mummy remains preserved in his burial chamber, is the most well-known. But this is by far the least impressive. The majority of the other tombs are, in fact, far more remarkable.

On your route to the Valley of the Kings, be sure to stop at the Colossi of Memnon. These two enormous sculptures, each of which is carved from a single block of stone and weighs up to 650 tonnes, each portray the Pharaoh Amenhotep III.

TEMPLE OF THE DEAD IN HATSHEPSUT

The beautiful Mortuary Temple honoring Queen Hatshepsut's life is close to the Valley of the Kings. This stunning temple has amazing illustrations of colorful hieroglyphs that vividly depict the commercial successes of Queen Hatshepsut. I especially liked the scenes when vessels were carrying a variety of imported items, such as exotic flora and

animals from Africa.

Recommendation: If you have time, the Medinet Habu, also known as the Mortuary Temple of Ramses III, is another fantastic addition to the West Bank.

SLEPER TAKE A TRAIN OR FLIGHT TO CAIRO

It's time to catch the sleeper train back to Cairo after a fantastic and exciting nine days of touring around Egypt. Being that you will likely be somewhat worn out by this point, the Luxor train station is more orderly than the Cairo one.

Additionally, if you'd choose, you may still travel back to Cairo. Within 15 minutes of the city, Luxor has an international airport.

ITINERARY FOR DAY 10: CAIRO - EGYPTIAN MUSEUM
I return to Cairo on my last day of travel in Egypt for one more day of sightseeing! This time, however, the emphasis will be on the city's top attractions, with an examination of the fascinating mingling of cultures that have built this amazing city for millennia.

LOCATIONS IN CAIRO

On this Egypt tour, Cairo is the focus both times, with less emphasis placed on the wonders of the West Bank. Therefore, it doesn't matter whether you stay in Giza or not.

Here are a few excellent choices for accommodations in Cairo.

The greatest 5-star luxury resort on the Nile is the Four Seasons Hotel Cairo at Nile Plaza. At this incredible hotel with two pools, spas, a gym, a hot tub, a massage parlor, and even its salon, you can experience 5-star luxury and celebrity treatment.

The Safir Hotel Cairo is a mid-range establishment that provides air-conditioned luxury rooms with access to a spa, a pool, and a gym. It is situated in the center of Cairo. The Nile River is only a 10-minute walk from the hotel. The Egyptian Museum and the Clock Tower can both be reached on foot from Holy Sheet Hostel, a great option for budget-conscious travelers. Every morning, a la carte breakfast is offered, which is ideal for individuals who wish to fuel up before spending the day visiting Cairo.

MORE ON BOOKING.COM

MUSEUM OF EGYPT (MUSEUM OF EGYPTIAN ANTIQUITIES)

It's best to visit the Egyptian Museum last so that you can fully enjoy its history and wonderful artifacts. You should now have a thorough grasp of ancient Egyptian history after seeing some of its most important sites.

The greatest ancient relics from Egypt are kept in this museum, which is the oldest in the Middle East. The King Tutankhamun exhibit, which includes the young king's iconic golden headpiece and coffin, was the

highlight for me.

Advice: The Grand Egyptian Museum, often known as the Giza Museum, is now being built in Egypt. It will be the biggest archaeological museum in the world once it opens!

THE HANGING CHURCH AND COPTIC CAIRO

Old Cairo includes Coptic Cairo, which has several churches and historical landmarks such as the Coptic Museum, the Greek Church of St. George, the Hanging Church,

and the Babylon Fortress.

One of the oldest buildings in Egypt, the spectacular Hanging Church, was one of the stops on our trip with TravelTalk. It got its name since it was built and hung on a wall of the Babylon Fortress in the fourth century.

THE MOHAMMAD ALI MOSQUE

I'm sure you've previously seen the magnificent mosque of Mohammad Ali if you've looked at the skyline of Cairo. The biggest mosque in Egypt built in the Ottoman architectural style, it has magnificent minarets and exquisitely adorned walls and domes.

The mosque's exterior offers stunning views of Cairo's surroundings. You may even see the Great Pyramids in the distance on a clear day.

BAZAR KHAN EL-KHALILI

The famed Khan El-Khalili Bazaar, the oldest bazaar (souq) in the Middle East, is the destination on this Egypt itinerary.
Explore the maze-like streets and hone your bartering skills. Tourists may buy nearly every kind of gift at this well-known market!

I also took the opportunity to have my last supper of delectable koshari and falafel while sitting in one of the old cafés and seeing the crowds of people trickling through the ancient streets.

ADDITIONS AND MODIFICATIONS TO THE EGYPT ITINERARY

I hope that this fantastic Egypt itinerary has motivated you to go to the country of the pharaohs and see all of its historic sites!
Even though 10 days in Egypt is a sufficient amount of time to explore many of its attractions, the reality is that this itinerary only touches the surface of what this nation has to offer.

I've included a couple of additional sections below for you to look at. Many of them may be added to this well-known Egypt tourism circuit, either before or after, according to distances.

THE PENINSULA OF SINAI

Just east of Cairo, the Sinai Peninsula is the peninsula with an upside-down diamond form that is trapped between Africa and the

Middle East.

For the opportunity to participate in Red Sea diving of the highest caliber, many tourists go to the Sinai Peninsula. Sharm el-Sheikh, a resort area with excellent diving, and Dahab, a laid-back backpacker town famous for its Blue Hole and nearby Blue Lagoon, are two well-liked tourist destinations in Sinai.

Many visitors to the Sinai Peninsula also want to climb Mount Sinai, which is said to be the biblical peak where Moses was given the 10 commandments.

Most visitors take a flight to Sharm el-Sheikh to get to Sinai. However, other buses go often from Cairo.

SOUTH RED SEA AND HURGHADA

Popular beach destination Hurghada is located on the Red Sea's southern coast. Since Hurghada offers a laid-back, resort-style atmosphere to unwind before taking a flight back to their home countries, many people choose to visit it after traveling in Egypt.

Hurghada, like Sharm el-Sheikh, has its airport, making it a simple place to get to from Cairo. Hurghada is a fantastic location to earn your open-water certification and is also known for its world-class scuba diving.

For the opportunity to swim with wild dolphins, which frequent this area of the

Red Sea, many people travel here.

ALEXANDRIA

Alexandria, an Egyptian port city on the Mediterranean Sea that was established by Alexander the Great, previously served as Egypt's capital.

The modern Bibliotheca Alexandrina, the Kom el-Shoqafa Catacombs, and the well-known Ras el-Tin Palace are just a few of Alexandria's attractions. However, most people just go to Alexandria for a day excursion from Cairo since they would rather spend some time by the Red Sea.

BLACK DESERT

The white chalk formations that dominate the terrain gave the White Desert, which is

in Western Egypt, its name. Although it is

now a relatively desolate wasteland, the fossils, shells, and salt deposits show that it was once entirely submerged.

The White Desert often receives one day on travelers' Egypt itineraries, although several tour operators also arrange camping and glamping in this area.

CRUISE THE NILE

I'm sure you've come across several Nile Cruises if you've been looking into Egypt's

trip possibilities.

The majority of the overland sections between Aswan and Luxor are now replaced by this. Numerous of the attractions mentioned in our travel guide will still be visited on these cruises. Just be careful to double-check the items since many do not include everything.

There are other 2, 3, 4, or 5-day cruises you may add in between days 3 and 8 of this itinerary if the Nile cruise seems like a better choice. Although I haven't personally taken one, TravelTalk offers a Nile Cruise option that seems like a fantastic deal.

No, Cairo is not a port of departure for an Egypt cruise.

This whole 10-day Egypt itinerary is now complete. I hope that helped prepare you for what to anticipate when traveling to Egypt.

This particular Itinerary was written by my wife when she and my kids traveled to Egypt in October, 2020. I couldn't join them then due to some emergency so I decided to include it as an optional itinerary for a family trip to Egypt. Hope it is useful.

THE ULTIMATE ITINERARY GUIDE FOR A FAMILY TRIP WITH KIDS

Several thoughts on organizing a family vacation to Egypt. When we visited Egypt in October, Mateo and Rapheal, our twins, were about 2.5 years old. Egypt is a fantastic, really intriguing nation to visit, but there may sometimes be some difficult times if you bring kids there.

You must continuously balance the urge to see more places with the reality of strolling at 1 pm in the scorching heat, maybe while carrying a youngster on your neck, back, or arm, when the temperature is above 30 degrees in October. It is not a very clean nation; but, with kids, you are constantly washing your hands and face to kill some germs, so I wasn't surprised by this. Most people who have been to Egypt claim that it is not especially clean. Additionally, there is sand everywhere, and what could be more appealing to toddlers than to play with or even eat sand? If you are comfortable traveling with young children, you will quickly adjust, relax, and simply give yourself more time to see the various locations. Plan to spend a few days at the shore after your family's trip to Egypt, where the sand, sun, and memories you make there will last a lifetime. This section contains my finest pointers and recommendations about how to make a family trip to Egypt memorable.

As you can see, certain things are missing from a 10-day vacation to Egypt. Time in Luxor is just enough for a brief look, but I believe a Nile cruise is essential when you are there, so I chose to sacrifice other activities to fit it in.

To fully use the 10 days, this plan implies an early arrival and a late departure.

Day One of Egypt's Schedule: The Pyramids

Upon arrival in Cairo, your 10-day trip to Egypt will begin. I advise you to stay in Giza during your time in Cairo so you may take in the magnificence of the Pyramids. When you arrive, be transferred to your hotel in Giza, where you can quickly freshen yourself before starting the day. Personally, my family and I stayed in the Marriott Mena House (more info later). You may go to the main ticket office for the Pyramids by walking for about five minutes from there.

Egypt began a digitalization process to enable everyone to purchase tickets online and shorten lines at the most popular attraction, but as of the beginning of 2021, it is still not complete (maybe due to the worldwide pandemic?). There is a chance that there may be a little line at the ticket

counter in the meantime.

Finding the most recent pricing is often challenging, but you may check the entry fees for all Egyptian museums and archaeological sites here for the years 2020–2022. To promote repeat international tourists, the Minister of Tourism and Antiquities will lower the cost of the majority of sites starting in the summer of 2020. The following are the typical rates for international visitors to the most popular sights (the government has dramatically increased these fees in recent years):

Area of the Giza Plateau 200 EGP (£9.30, €10.50, and $12.80)

400 EGP (€21.0, £18.60, $23.60) The Great Pyramid

Pyramid of Khafre 100 EGP (5.20 EUR, 4.65 GBP, 6.40 USD)

600 EGP ($31.30; £28.00; $38.20) gets you access to the Great Pyramid, the Boat Museum, and public entry.

It is prohibited to bring cameras within the Pyramids. You may leave your camera in the security officer's care at the entry; when you depart, 5 EGP will suffice as a tip. Keep your ticket handy since they will need it to match your camera. You may purchase a second ticket to carry the camera with you to other sites/museums. Although using our phones was not an issue at the Pyramids.

Bringing young children into the Pyramids

Be advised that there are two very long, narrow, steep, and crowded wooden slopes/stairs that must be climbed to reach the top chamber if you opt to see the Great Pyramids with young children (I highly suggest it, even if there isn't much to see inside). It becomes heated inside with little airflow.

Suggestions for seeing the Pyramids

Being so near to something so special and old gives walking about here a certain air of wonder. When we visited, the location wasn't especially crowded, and we were nearly by ourselves within the Great Pyramid.

Although the site is large, it is certainly feasible for an adult in excellent condition to walk around, travel from the Pyramids to the Sphinx, and, with a little more effort, even to the observation platform, even in the heat. 3–4 hours should be given.

It could be different if you are visiting the Pyramids with children, however.

OUR EXPERIENCE: We are in decent condition, but I'm not strong enough to carry a 16-kg toddler for an extended period while walking in the hot sun. We were harassed by touts who tried to sell us something or get us to ride a camel or horses from the minute we arrived (and even before).

We agreed to pay 300 EGP (total for 1 hour with 2 camels) to go to the observation point and then down to the Sphinx after deciding at some point to check whether any of them genuinely had any healthy-looking camels.

Before agreeing to anything with anybody, ask them to show you which camel or horse you are going to ride. Only accept if they seem well-fed and in excellent condition. There are many individuals and their animals surrounding the pyramids, and not all of them seem to be in good health.

HINT: If you ride a horse or a camel, make sure to negotiate the fee and the precise destination before you leave. They should hear it from you many times, including the actual guide. Some of the pleasure of our camel trip was destroyed by the guy who was driving it since he was trying to shorten it and pushed hard for more money.

You'll probably start to feel the desire for a nap once you get near the Sphinx. Take a cab back to the hotel, although if you are physically able, consider walking instead as taxis must navigate through often congested traffic.

Even though you came early, your day has probably already been strenuous enough; my advice is to ease off and unwind for the remainder of the day so you can prepare for a long day tomorrow.

DAY TWO ITINERARY FOR EGYPT: ONE DAY IN CAIRO

The whole second day is devoted to seeing Cairo. Cairo is a large city, so it could be difficult to decide what to visit in a single day, but these are the highlights.
You may take an Uber to the Coptic Cairo first thing in the morning for 64 EGP. One of the nicest spots to explore in Cairo is this charming little neighborhood, which is quite simple to navigate on foot.

You may see the Hanging Church, which may be the first Christian building in Egypt, as well as the Ben Ezra Synagogue, the Church of St. George, the St. Barbara Church, and the gorgeous Greek Orthodox cemetery. This tour lasts around two hours, but if you also want to see the Coptic

museum, you'll need additional time.

HINT: The sole dining establishment in the vicinity is a café where you may get modest snacks and beverages. If your children are finicky eaters, you should provide something. There are several more possibilities close to the Egyptian museum, which is the next destination.

You may take a second Uber from Coptic Cairo to the Egyptian Museum for 35 EGP. The benefit of visiting the Egyptian museum during lunchtime is that you will be inside during the warmest part of the day.

Tickets are available for purchase at the museum's entry. You may only carry your camera inside the museum if you purchase an additional ticket; be sure to purchase it at the same time as your admission ticket to avoid having to leave your camera at the door. A separate ticket is also necessary for the Mummies chamber. When you arrive at it, you may purchase it inside or at the door.

Here is a breakdown of costs:

200 EGP ($10.50, £9.30, or $12.80) is the entry price.

Room for mummies: 180 EGP ($9.40, £8.40, or £11.50).

300 EGP ($15.60, £14.00, or $19.20) is the cost of the combined ticket (admission and Mummy's room).

CAVEAT: Visiting this museum when in Egypt is a necessity, but I'm so happy that the new Museum (GEM) will soon be opening since the original Egyptian museum was, in my opinion, the worst letdown of our trip. I expected to see a location with outdated displays and in a state of transition, but I didn't anticipate it would be so subpar. Don't get me wrong, the items on show are incredible and intriguing genuine historical artifacts, however, they are dimly lit and sometimes lack explanations in English (or often no signage at all). The

Tutankhamun chamber and the Mummy's rooms are off-limits for photography.

A guided tour of the museum led by an Egyptologist would be quite beneficial if you want to fully appreciate the enormous artifacts that are on show there. You won't regret using that cash!

Take another Uber (27 EGP) when your museum tour is over to quickly check out the Khan el-Khalili market. This bazaar is wonderful for exploring for a while.
It is a crowded market with winding lanes with souvenirs of every kind. Always haggle the price and be sure to confirm that they are local rather than imported.

You may just eat something at the market or a nearby restaurant to round up your Cairo in a Day short trip. Another option is to dine at one of Cairo's upscale establishments to see a distinct aspect of the city. According to my study, you should choose "8" or "The

Birdcage," two upscale Chinese and Thai eateries. Unfortunately, I am unable to remark since we didn't know they didn't welcome children until we arrived! If you want to taste anything other than the local food, ask your hotel owner to phone and inquire since there aren't many other possibilities outside of Cairo.

At this time, a cab ride back to the Mena residence should be quick and cost around 80 EGP.

3rd day's itinerary in Egypt: SAQQARA and food tour

Try to arrive early since there is no shelter from the intense heat; Saqqara is an amazing burial site and requires a whole half day.

The oldest pyramid in the world is the stepped Pyramid of Djoser, but it's not the only remarkable structure. You must pass through a magnificent limestone wall that is more than 10 meters high to get to the spot. You will pass through a massive colonnade after entering the entrance that has been almost unchanged for about 5,000 years (the pillars are now covered with a concrete roof to protect them)

It may be monotonous, but I must reiterate that visiting Egypt will transport you back in time. Be careful that certain tombs shut for an hour at 1 o'clock (of course, I entered one of them just as the guard closed the entrance to it:

OUR EXPERIENCE: Because we arrived late, the site was too hot for us to tour more than a little portion of it. When we arrived, we requested the Uber driver to wait for us. Throughout our exploration, he kept the route open on the app. The trip from Giza to Saqqara was around 50 kilometers, and we had Uber for about 3 hours. We spent $14.

(261 EGP, but the fare was 1.5x higher than usual)

Another location where having a guide is beneficial to appreciate the magnificence of the sand is Saqqara. The entry fee is as follows:

180 EGP (€9.40, £8.40, $11.50) gets you to access to the site and the Imhotep Museum

(€5.20, £4.65, $6.40) Pyramid of Djoser 100 EGP

Noble graves at the New Kingdom Cemetery cost 140 EGP ($9.00, €7.30, and £6.50).

Mereruka's Tomb 80 EGP (€4.20, £3.80, $5.10)

Eating tour

It's time for a cuisine tour once you've cooled down at your hotel (perhaps with a dip in the pool).

A fantastic option for the family vacation is a cuisine tour. It allows both of you and them to sample new meals without committing to a complete meal. You could feel overrun in Cairo by the diversity of local establishments. Without local expertise or additional time, it may be challenging to find the hidden jewels in your area, even with a thorough study. The two women behind Bellies en Route do a fantastic job of explaining the history and significance of Egyptian food to you while also sharing with you its culinary heritage.

Our interactions with them were flawless. They advised us to schedule a private trip since, with young children, we could customize it to meet our requirements and be flexible.

You will spend over 4 hours exploring Cairo's back alleys, seeing new sights, and sampling foods you may never have heard of before! They were also quite helpful from a practical standpoint since we had a private tour. Our tour guide for the culinary portion of the trip, Laila, greeted us in front of the Egyptian Museum and was quite gracious in allowing us to leave our bags in her vehicle while we explored. Heading back to Giza merely to pick up the bags didn't make sense since we were going directly to the airport after the trip.

Cairo is where the gastronomic journey concludes. It's time to depart for Aswan (there are usually quite late flights). You can simply grab an Uber (around 150 EGP) from downtown Cairo. Be mindful of the traffic; getting there in the evening might take up to an hour and a half.

Day Four of Egypt's Schedule: ASWAN

Aswan is the beginning of a new journey. Because of how little space there is, you may go straight from arrivals to the street. Late at night, there is little to no traffic, the air is pleasant, and the gentle breeze instantly relaxes you and puts a smile on your face.

You might choose to stay in Aswan or the Nubian settlement beside the Nile just outside the city. The Kato Dool Nubian resort was where we stayed. (More details after the schedule)

Spend some time exploring the Nubian village in the morning. As you go about, you'll be greeted with colorful homes and kind people. You won't often experience too much pressure to purchase anything since they are most used to visitors who come on organized trips. Take advantage of a tasty regional meal served at your guesthouse or visit the Kato Doll for delicious cuisine, feet in the sand, and a river view.

Go to Aswan in the afternoon. After our guesthouse owner arranged for us to take a 250 EGP motorboat transport, we arrived after 10 minutes and much kid-led hilarity.

Explore the city, the market, and the Nile on foot. You might go to Elephantine Island or simply relax and enjoy life here. You may take a public boat across the Nile (near the garden on the waterfront) to go to Elephantine Island, or you can embark on a short felucca trip to cruise around it.

You might also try to go to the High Dam or the Philae Temple.

Enjoy a beverage at the venerable Old Cataract Hotel as the sun sets. Since there is no Uber accessible, you will need to negotiate a price with one of the numerous taxi drivers in the area to return to the Nubian hamlet.

OUR EXPERIENCE: We relaxed for a little while in Aswan. We loved our time in the Nubian village as well as our strolls around

Aswan's Souq and gardens. We would have been delighted to have a martini at the Old Cataract, but when we arrived at the gate, we were informed that the hotel was completely booked for a private event and that it was off-limits to other guests.

If you slow down and spend some time in Aswan, you may find it tough to leave. Aswan is one of those places that you may pass by and assume there is nothing to do or see.

Day 5's itinerary in Egypt: NILE CRUISE

Another adventure—a voyage down the Nile in Egypt—begins on day 5.

To sail the Nile, you have a choice of two different kinds of boats. There is the traditional Dahabiya as well as the customary huge boat used on cruises. Small sailing vessels called Dahabiya often only have 5 or 6 berths. The Dahabiya will let you calm down and unwind while providing a new perspective on life on the Nile. This 10-day itinerary for Egypt will take a Dahabiya boat tour along the Nile into account.

We made our reservations via Djed, and everything went well. Four times every week, they sail both ways on the Nile. Verify again where the cruise departs on that particular day of the week when putting up your itinerary for Egypt.

Esna to Aswan (Luxor). 3 nights in Downriver for as little as €570 each (double occupancy)

From Luxor (Esna) to Aswan. 4 nights for up to 760 euros per person (double occupancy)

Children ages 1 to 4 stay free when sharing a cabin with adults; children ages 5 to 12 receive a 20% discount. Transfers between Aswan and Luxor, all entrance fees, a guide who is always with you, full board (including afternoon tea), all drinks (aside from alcoholic beverages), and wi-fi are all included in the price.

There is ample room on a sailing vessel for everyone to unwind and take in the scenery. a hammock, many lounge chairs, floor cushions, and sunbeds. Although the Dahabiya is a tiny boat, the mood is usually calm and laid back since there are never more than 12 people on board.

The crew is not unprepared for passengers traveling with children; they are always willing to assist and sometimes even engage in play with the children. It is reasonable to worry that your children could disrupt the mood of other visitors, but as long as they are well-behaved, you shouldn't worry.
You'll be picked up at about 9 am and transported to a Dahabiya boat where your

Nile tour will begin! It's like walking into the set of an Agatha Christie film when you board!

I was very happy! Despite not being a lover of cruises, I've always wanted to take a trip to the Nile, and after much study and uncertainty about taking a family with young children, my dream has come true.
After boarding, you will meet the other passengers, the staff, the captain, and the Egyptologist guide who will accompany you on the trip. Before the sailing begins, the guide will give you a quick overview of the three days you will spend together.

On the top deck, meals are typically served all at once.

Temple of Kom Ombo and Crocodile Museum

You will go to the Kom Ombo Temple on the first day in the afternoon. This remarkable twin temple honors the Nile Gods Haroeris (Horus the Elder), the falcon deity Haroeris, and the local crocodile god Sobek.

For its design, it is regarded as remarkable and distinctive. Two identical but separate parts are devoted to the two Gods.

The Crocodile Museum is located close to the Kom Ombo Temple. The about 300 mummified crocodiles discovered nearby are preserved in a wonderfully cool tiny museum.

It is quite useful to use a Dahabiya to go to this location. Due to their modest size and ability to anchor practically anywhere, dahabiya can access areas that larger cruise ships cannot. The distance to the temple is short when using a Dahabiya.

NILE CRUISE IN THE DAY 6 EGYPT ITINERARY

After an early breakfast, you will see the sandstone quarries at Gebel el-Silsila and the rock-cut chapels of Horemheb, Seti I, Ramses II, and Merenptah. When you consider that the sandstone quarry provided the stone for the majority of Egypt's important temples, it is an astonishing sight. To get to their goal, every stone had to travel on the Nile.

On the second day, the wind increased a little throughout the day, so we were able to continue with some sailing. (Typically, a motor boat far enough away from the Dahabiya boat to not make much noise)

You may make a wonderful pit stop at a little beach in the afternoon to have a dip in the Nile.

A parasite in the stagnant water of the Nile may be quite hazardous, so use caution. This danger does not exist when the river current is greater, but always heed the boat captain's instructions on where to swim. If the weather is good, the crew will set up an unforgettable dinner on the serene riverbanks the following night.

Day Seven's Egypt Schedule: NILE CRUISE

The Edfu Temple will be the first destination after breakfast. This Horus-focused temple is not located at the Nile's edge. You'll need a horse-drawn carriage to get there. Everything is set up so that you cannot make a decision based just on how healthy the animals seem. Sadly, ours was tiny, which made the beginning rather depressing.

The beautiful temple is one of the finest kept. 200 years ago, it was buried in sand, which preserved it. It could be extremely crowded, and to go in, you'll have to go past a line of sellers displaying their goods. There is another intriguing and somewhat less crowded place in the afternoon. One of the most important and oldest archaeological sites on the Nile is El Kab, the former town of Nekheb. You will see some of the tombs carved into the cliffs as well as the temple ruins.

You will arrive in Esna in the evening, where the Dahabiya will spend the night. You have the option to go outside and do some exploring. In my perspective, anchoring near a city with its commotion and noise somewhat destroys the mood of the previous evening.

Additionally, now is the time to have an envelope ready with a gratuity for the captain, crew, and guide. Though it is not required, our guide advised us to do this (who also gives you the envelopes).

DAY 8 ITINERARY FOR EGYPT: LUXOR

After breakfast, the cruise will end at about 10 am. As I indicated at the beginning, there isn't much time allotted to Luxor in my 10-day schedule for Egypt to create room for some leisurely time on the Red Sea beaches.

Request a breakfast that starts early since you need to check out of Dahabiya at about 7 am. The Red Sea may be reached by hiring a vehicle to transport you around Luxor throughout the day. We agreed on paying €130 + €30 for the guide who joined us on the tour when we made our reservation via the same firm we used for the Nile cruise.

HINT: A cab from Luxor to the Red Sea requires police permission, which must often be secured the day before the trip. Remember this since it could be challenging to locate a last-minute transportation option. If you want to remain in Luxor for a longer period, I'm certain that you may negotiate a much better rate with many drivers.

You may explore the Valley of the Kings, the Memnon colossi, the Karnak Temple, and the Temple of Hatshepsut during your brief stay in Luxor.

<u>The Kings' Valley</u>

The Valley of the Kings is a fantastic location that transports you to a different planet in a different dimension.
This is also the first location where you will see a lot of tourists; they are not a cause for concern, but they are unquestionably more numerous than at the other locations you visited. You will notice that Luxor is more crowded because many visitors taking Red Sea vacations choose to make the long day trip there.

When you first arrive, the scene is rather unimpressive, but since everything is taking place underground, don't worry; as soon as you enter the first tomb, you'll be rewarded with breathtaking sights.

Tickets price:
Site entry fee including access to 3 Tombs 240 EGP (£11.20, €12.50, and $15.30)

300 EGP ($15.60, £14.00, or $19.20) Tutankhamun tomb

Ramses VI 100 EGP (5.20 EUR, 4.65 GBP, 6.40 USD)

300 EGP ($15.60, £14.00, or $19.20) for a camera ticket

Except for those tombs that are closed (some are "resting," others are being repaired, etc.) and those tombs that call for an additional ticket, the general access ticket allows you to enter into three of your preferred tombs. You can only take photographs in the 3 tombs you choose with the admission ticket (there are no images allowed in Tutankhamun's tomb), and you must pay an additional 300EGP for each camera you use.

Which tombs in the Valley of the Kings should you visit?

Although the tomb buildings seemed to be identical, none of them were. The King Mummy would slumber in a sarcophagus at the end of a long tunnel with storage chambers around it. Other common features include steps or a steep downhill approach.
We used the public access ticket to see the tombs of Ramses III, IV, and IX. Ramses IV was very impressive. To access the tombs of Ramses V and VI and Tutankhamun, we purchased an additional 2 tickets.

Even though I heard Tutankhamun's tomb was one of the less stunning ones and that it was photo-unfriendly, we nevertheless made the decision to go inside. Although I can't advise spending money on it, the Tutankhamun mythology has always had such a significant impact on Egypt's current history that many people just can't ignore it. That his Mummy is still in his tomb resting (well preserved beneath a nice glass box) is a little unsettling, but it also fuels the mystique.

Except for the obvious need to enter the tombs, the site is completely accessible with a stroller. A pram might be useful because it requires some walking to get from the parking lot to the entrance (although a small electric train is available); if you are with a guide, they can watch over it while you enter the tombs.

OUR EXPERIENCE: The tombs we visited were all very close to the entrance and very easy for Mateo and Rapheal to walk; however, I would have liked to visit

Merenptah tomb, but our guide suggested that it might be too difficult for them because it has a lot of steep steps. Looking at the structure now, it doesn't seem so steep, but of course, I trusted our guide.

One of my favorite parts of the trip was the Valley of the Kings, although I wasn't adequately prepared. I'm delighted with what we saw, but I advise you to do some prior study on the tombs you want to visit.

Following your visit to the Valley of the Kings, you will go to the Karnak Temple with a quick detour to view the Colossus of Memnon.

Temple of Karnak

The Karnak Temple is amazing. It is, in my opinion, among Egypt's best locations. If you stay in Luxor, you may return at night to see the magnificent music and light spectacle. You can't help but feel like you're in the "Death on the Nile" scene as you meander among the 134 enormous pillars (if you have seen it). It is just astounding.

The entry fee is 200 EGP, which also covers admission to the open museum in Karnak (costs €10.50, £9.30, or $12.80).

The Karnak Temple is essentially a collection of many temples constructed over 2000 years. It is so amazing that it could be overpowering. Be advised that the Avenue of the Sphinxes, which runs parallel to the Luxor Temple, was formerly a very lengthy avenue created by the sphinxes. The primary structure is the enormous Temple of Amun. It has been updated by several Pharaohs and is still mighty and intimidating.

All around, remnants from several further sites are still discernible in varying degrees of conservation. Don't forget to see the lake, the Temple of Khonsu, the Temple of Ramses II, and the little Temple of Osiris.

When a knowledgeable guide can describe what you are seeing to you properly, another sight where you can undoubtedly enjoy much more of such an old civilization is the Karnak Temple.

You must depart Luxor at approximately 3 o'clock to move to the Red Sea. Even though the distance is less than 250 km, the transfer must travel a longer route that takes approximately 5 hours.

ITINERARY FOR DAYS 9–10 IN EGYPT: RED SEA

The final two days will go by very slowly as we enjoy the beach, eat delicious food, go kayaking, play on the playground, read, and watch the sunrise. The ideal end to a 10-day vacation in Egypt!

OUR EXPERIENCE: We chose to unwind by choosing to stay at the Radisson Blu Resort (see more below). You may leave the resort and tour Quseir, but we chose to disconnect and just take in the sun, beach, and water. We all had a great time there when Mateo and Rapheal were 28 months old!

You should be able to connect from Hurghada to Cairo to take a flight home. El Quseir and Hurghada airport can be reached by car in about 90 minutes. You'll need a taxi, so ask your hotel to reserve one for you. Alternatively, ask one of the previous drivers; they'll undoubtedly know someone.

Adapt the itinerary for the 10 days in Egypt.

If you have more or less time, let's look at how to quickly modify this plan. If you are only in Egypt for a week, you will have to skip the Red Sea excursion and go straight from Cairo to the Nile cruise, skipping the stop in Aswan. In my opinion, three days in Cairo should be the absolute minimum to fully experience everything it has to offer and to get a taste of the local culture.

A schedule for one week in Egypt is shown below. As you can see, I advise you to include the Nile Cruise even in a 7-day schedule for Egypt.

EGYPT ITINERARY OPTION FOR 7 DAYS

Getting to Cairo

Cairo

Cairo

A Nile Cruise

A Nile Cruise

A Nile Cruise

Luxor

The plan below contains the greatest spots to visit in Egypt if you have a little more time to get there, allowing time for relaxation as well. You may choose to break the third day into two if you have two weeks in Egypt and want to spend an additional day in Cairo. After touring Saqqara on day 3, you may go to Dashur. You may explore Islamic Cairo in the morning on Day 4 and participate in the cuisine tour in the late afternoon. You'll spend an additional day or night in Aswan. You may utilize that time to plan a day excursion to Abu Simbel.

Your schedule for Luxor may be expanded to incorporate additional sightseeing if you have time. A hot air balloon flight is an option, and you may tour Hatshepsut's Temple, the Noble Tombs, the Medinet Habu Temple, and more!

The ideal schedule for Egypt to get a full picture of the nation is this one.

A 2-WEEK ITINERARY FOR EGYPT

Getting to Cairo

Cairo

Cairo

Cairo-Aswan, Aswan, Abu Simbel, Nile Cruise, A Nile Cruise, A Nile Cruise, Luxor, Luxor, Red Ocean, Red Ocean, Red Ocean.

Accommodations in Egypt

Cairo

Where to stay when you arrive is the first choice to be made when creating an Egypt vacation itinerary. The two primary choices are central Cairo or Giza (about 5 kilometers from Cairo, where the Pyramids are). While there, you'll sometimes visit locations in Cairo and occasionally ones closer to Giza.

If you make the right choices, you may wake up every morning in front of the last of the ancient world's seven wonders, even if there are no other noteworthy sites to visit in Giza other than the Pyramids (until the new GEM opens).

For this reason, I advise staying in Giza on a three-day itinerary for Cairo. We slept at the Marriott Mena House, a historic hotel that is still a part of the Marriott brand. In 1886, the hotel debuted as a spectacular oriental palace. The palace has had several renovations and additions since that period, including a new wing. Although it is now a modern complex, it still exudes luxury and charm. The rooms are spacious and have a lovely balcony where you can unwind. A Pyramid view is offered by many of them. Additionally, the hotel may set up cribs in your space. Even with two, we had ample room to walk about without difficulty.

In addition to a small children's pool, there is a lovely swimming pool. Two distinct eateries serve either international or Indian cuisine. There is a large and diverse breakfast buffet. You just need 25,000 Marriott points to stay here if you are a point collector.

The Egypt Pyramids Inn or the Pyramids Guest House are two options to consider if you're searching for something a bit less expensive. These are more compact, family-run accommodations on the Sphinx side. Some of the rooms have views of the Pyramids, and both have fantastic roof terraces with breathtaking panoramas of the Giza plateau.

Aswan

Although I would have wanted to stay at the Sofitel Legend Old Cataract in Aswan, we had a great time at the Kato Dool Nubian resort. Unfortunately, the best hotels in town were completely occupied because a well-known Egyptian was getting married.

If you can afford the Old Cataract, you may imagine yourself as Agatha Christie and draw ideas for your next book.

In front of Elephantine Island, on the banks of the Nile, is where you'll find the hotel. Magnificent Nile views can be found in many rooms and suites.

One indoor pool and one outdoor pool are available. With international and oriental options, four restaurants have something for everyone. If you feel particularly energetic, you can work out in the fitness center before unwinding in the sauna, hammam, and hot tub in the spa.

Resort at Kato Dool Nubian

The wonderful family-run Kato Dool Nubian retreat is a hotel. Although it would be a stretch to refer to it as a resort, it is a great site to learn about the Nubian culture.

The tiny homes are situated right next to the Nile. Although they are quite clean, the rooms are not those of a five-star hotel. However, if you need to add two cots, they are a little on the small side.

It's nice to open the door in the morning to the peaceful river vista and have a satisfying breakfast at one of the colorful tables set up on the beach.

Additionally, they provide the option to have lunch and supper. Even in its simplicity, the nighttime ambiance is beautiful and soothing, and the food is excellent.

El Quseir, the Red Sea

You will have a wide range of accommodations to choose from near the Red Sea, ranging from 5-star resorts to more modest guesthouses. The value at the Radisson Blu Resort is unrivaled.

One of those spots where you could contemplate returning simply to unwind is the Radisson Blu Resort. Since there is nothing else around, I advise taking advantage of their full or half-board options.

The resort is huge and offers both a tranquil lagoon and a pretty long stretch of beach. You won't feel out of place since everything is tastefully merged into the surroundings and there is no pretentiousness.

There are several varieties of rooms. Of course, those closest to the shore, where you can see the dawn, are the finest. A large pool and a smaller, covered kids' pool are also present. The lagoon and the playground are both excellent for kids.

Top sight attractions

Egypt, the former home of the Pharaohs, is a fascinating tourist destination with glittering buildings and tombs that awe travelers. Though not all of it consists of historical monuments and tourist destinations. All sorts of tourists may find something to do in Egypt thanks to the enormous expanses of desert that are perfect for 4WD excursions, the world-class coral reefs and wrecks in the Red Sea, and cruises on the renowned Nile River.

Beachgoers seeking some sun can travel to the Sinai or the Red Sea Coast, while archaeological buffs will appreciate Luxor.

For city slickers, Cairo is the unrivaled megalopolis, while Siwa oasis and the southern town of Aswan provide a taste of the leisurely pace of the countryside.

Egypt provides travelers the possibility to design itineraries that include culture, adventure, and leisure all in one trip, as I have already done in this book. This is because there is so much to see and do there. Now, in addition to the locations included in the itineraries, you may organize your tour using my list of Egypt's best sites and attractions.

1. Giza Pyramids

The Pyramids of Giza are one of the most well-known sights in the world and the final remaining example of one of the Seven Wonders of the Ancient World. These tombs of the Pharaohs Cheops (Khufu), Chephren (Khafre), and Mycerinus (Menkaure), guarded by the enigmatic Sphinx, have fascinated visitors throughout history and are typically at the top of most visitors' lists of tourist attractions to see in Egypt and frequently the first sight they head to after landing.

These megalithic monuments to deceased pharaohs, which are located on the outskirts of Cairo's sprawling desert, are still a breathtaking sight today and an unquestionable highlight of any journey to Egypt.

2. Temples & Tombs of Luxor

The Upper Egyptian town of Luxor features a ton of tourist attractions, including the Valley of the Kings, Karnak Temple, and Memorial Temple of Hatshepsut. Ancient Thebes, the seat of the New Kingdom pharaohs, is home to more attractions than the majority of people can see in a single trip.

The present city, with its bustling souq, the two temples of Karnak and Luxor, as well as the museum, are all located on the east bank of Luxor. The bulk of Luxor's tourist attractions is located on the west bank, which boasts so many tombs and temples that it has been dubbed the largest open-air museum in the world. You'll understand why Luxor continues to captivate historians and archaeologists after spending a few days here examining the vibrant tomb wall paintings and marveling at the enormous columns in the temples.

3. Taking a Nile cruise

The Nile is what defines Egypt. A multi-day voyage down this renowned canal, which saw the beginning of the Pharaonic period, is a popular tourist activity in Egypt. One of Egypt's most serene sights is dawn and sunset over the date palm-lined river banks, which are backed by dunes. The Nile is also the most soothing way to view the temples that dot the banks of the river on the path between Luxor and Aswan.

The Temple of Kom Ombo and Edfu's Temple of Horus, where all the major cruise boats stop, are the two most well-known attractions on a Nile cruise.

However, if you want a slower-paced, less crowded experience and don't mind a little bit of "roughing it," you can also cruise the Nile aboard a felucca, one of Egypt's ancient lateen-sailed wooden boats, which also lets you choose your schedule. However, feluccas may only be rented for multi-day journeys from Aswan, where the majority of cruise ship itineraries leave.

4. Aswan

Aswan, located among the Nile's sweeping bends, is the calmest town in all of Egypt. This is the ideal area to stop, rest for a few days, and take in the laid-back environment since it is surrounded by orange-hued dunes.

Take the riverboat to Elephantine Island and see the Nubian settlements' vibrant alleys. Then take a camel to St. Simeon's Desert Monastery on Aswan's East Bank.

After that, unwind at a riverside café while observing the feluccas with lateen sails cruising by.

Make sure you take a felucca at dusk to cruise the islands of Aswan. The most popular and tranquil method to see the attractions in Aswan is without a doubt this. There are many historical monuments nearby and several temples, including Philae Temple on its island, but one of the most well-liked things to do in Aswan is to unwind and observe river life.

5. Abu Simbel

Even though the nation is covered with temples, Abu Simbel is unique. This is Ramses II's huge temple, which is guarded by enormous statues outside and lavishly decorated within with murals. In addition to being renowned for its enormous size, Abu Simbel is also well-known for the amazing engineering feat performed by UNESCO in the 1960s, which saw the relocation of the entire temple from its original location to prevent it from being submerged by the Aswan dam's rising waters.

Nowadays, visiting Abu Simbel is as much about celebrating the success of the global campaign to preserve the temple complex as it is about staring in amazement at Ramses II's magnificent construction efforts.

6. The Red Sea dive

Divers swimming in the Red Sea's stunning underwater scenery

As interesting as the temples and tombs on land are other realms that lie under the Red Sea. The Red Sea's coral reefs are well-known among scuba divers for their soft coral displays as well as their abundance of marine life, which includes everything from vibrant reef fish and nudibranchs to sharks, dolphins, turtles, rays, and even dugongs. Sharm el-Sheikh, located on the Sinai Peninsula and closest to the reefs of Ras Mohammed National Park and the Straits of Tiran, is the most well-known town to base oneself in for divers.

Go to Hurghada or El Gouna on the Red Sea coast to dive into the Straits of Gubal dive

sites. For expert divers, Marsa Alam is the

closest base for exploring Egypt's "deep south" dive sites.

The Red Sea is a popular location for wreck diving in addition to having fish and coral. The Thistlegorm, a British WWII cargo ship that was being used to resupply Allied forces when it was attacked by the Germans in 1941, is the most well-known wreck.

Due to the massive load of vehicles, motorcycles, and WWII memorabilia that can be seen both within the ship and dispersed on the seabed surrounding the wreck, the site is now rated by divers as one of the top five wreck dives in the world. Both Sharm el-Sheikh and Hurghada conduct dive boat tours to the wreck.

7. Investigate Islamic Cairo

Mosques, madrassas (Islamic institutions of study), and monuments from the Fatimid through the Mameluke periods are jammed into the evocative, winding alleyways of the capital's Islamic Cairo area.

Here is where you'll discover Khan el-maze-like Khalili's souq, where coppersmiths and other artists still maintain little studios and booths crammed with spices, linens, and perfume.

The market is surrounded by a maze of lanes that are home to some of the most exquisitely preserved Islamic structures.

There is a ton of history to discover here. Visit the magnificent Sultan Hassan Mosque and the Al-Azhar Mosque, and be sure to climb to the top of the venerable medieval gate of Bab Zuweila for the greatest views of the neighborhood dotted with minarets.

8. Beach Life in South Sinai

On the Sinai Peninsula, in Egypt's South Sinai area, there is a beach for every kind of vacationer. A resort town in the manner of Europe, Sharm el-Sheikh is crammed with five-star hotels, foreign eateries, and a ton of entertainment choices. Many of the resorts in this area cater to families for one- or two-week sun and beach getaways, making it popular among Europeans traveling in the winter months.

Dahab is a laid-back beach town with a backpacker's heart that values the desert as much as it does the sea. It is famous for its inexpensive diving packages and for the lagoon beach area where windsurfing and kitesurfing are the most popular sports.
The bamboo hut retreats along the coast, between the border town of Taba and the port town of Nuweiba, providing total get-away-from-it-all respites from life and back-to-basics beach living.

9. Saqqara

Saqqara's ruins and pyramid

The Giza Pyramids are well-known, but Egypt also has more pyramids under its sleeve. Saqqara, a large necropolis of tombs and pyramids that was used throughout each period of pharaonic power, is a day's journey from Cairo. Its Old Kingdom Step Pyramid, which demonstrates how Ancient Egyptian builders expanded their technical expertise to ultimately produce a genuine pyramid form, is its most famous feature.

However, there is much more to see than just the Step Pyramid, as some of the nearby tombs, like the Mastaba of Ti, include some of the best tomb art you will ever see.
The Red Pyramid and the Bent Pyramid are located in the nearby Dahshur pyramid site, and both should be seen while at Saqqara.

10. Museum of Egypt

One of the greatest museum collections in the world, Cairo's Egyptian Museum is a treasure trove of the Pharaonic civilization.

There are a bewildering number of exhibits housed in the dilapidated pink palace in central Cairo.

It's a disorganized space with little labeling and a serious lack of chronological order. An amazing piece of antique art or statues may be found around every corner here, which would be the focus of any museum.

The haul of golden artifacts recovered from Tutankhamun's tomb in the Valley of the Kings is the centerpiece of the museum. Travelers should be aware that the wealth of the Egyptian Museum is now being moved to the brand-new Grand Egyptian Museum (GEM), which will be located in Giza, close to the pyramids, and is provisionally scheduled to open in November 2022 (after years of delays).

The totality of Tutankhamun's treasures, many of which have been held in storage for years, will now be fully on display, thanks to the GEM's provision of this world-class collection with a deserving exhibit.

11. Black Desert

White Desert National Park, located south of Bahariya Oasis in the Western Desert, is Egypt's quirkiest natural marvel. Here, bizarrely sculpted chalk pinnacles and enormous boulders tower over the desert plateau, giving the impression that icebergs have been stranded in the middle of a sandy environment. This very beautiful area, which resembles something from a science fiction film, is a favored location for 4WD desert excursions and overnight camping since Bahariya Oasis makes it simple to arrange both activities.

Anyone who has had their fill of temples and tombs will appreciate this breathtaking natural environment, while dessert enthusiasts and explorers will find it to be the ultimate odd playground.

12. Alexandria

There aren't many places that can compare to Alexandria's history.
This seaside city, which was founded by Alexander the Great, was also the birthplace of Cleopatra and a razzmatazz renegade city of the Mediterranean for a long of its existence.

Alexandria's long Corniche seafront road leading to its fort (located on the site where its famous ancient lighthouse once sat) continues to be a popular summer destination for Egyptians and foreign visitors alike to capture cooling sea breezes even though there are currently few historical remnants of its illustrious past left to see. Here, underwater archaeological expeditions have added fascinating artifacts to Alexandria's museums. The great ancient library of Alexandria has been modernized as the Bibliotheca Alexandrina, and among the town's few historical sites is the eerie catacombs site.

13. Temple of Abydos

One of the most intriguing aesthetic artifacts from ancient Egypt is the Temple of Osiris at Abydos. The Seti I-built temple is located inside a sizable necropolis where active archeological investigations are taking place. Although there are many more temple ruins to explore in this area, the Temple of Osiris is the major draw for most tourists.

Some of the best relief art in Egypt may be seen in its hypostyle halls, which are decorated with papyrus-headed columns and have figures depicting the king and the gods of ancient Egypt. The temple is far less visited than the temple sites at Luxor and the Nile-side temples to the south since it is located north of Luxor and off the usual cruise ship route. As a result, you frequently have the opportunity to explore the temple's halls alone or with just a few other visitors.

14. Sacred Oasis

Siwa is the peaceful antidote to the bustle of Egypt's cities, sitting alone in the westernmost corner of the Western Desert. One of the most stunning locations in the Western Desert is this lovely tiny oasis, which is flanked by date palm farms and several hot springs.

Siwa village is built around the remains of the Fortress of Shali, a massive mud-brick fortification that dominates the landscape. Throughout the larger oasis region are scattered temple ruins, notably the Temple of the Oracle, where Alexander the Great is reputed to have sought guidance. This is a great place to unwind and take it easy for a few days, and it also makes a great base for organizing excursions into the nearby desert.

15. The monastery of St. Catherine

St. Catherine's, one of the world's oldest monasteries, is located in the Sinai Peninsula's desert highlands, close to Mount Sinai, where it is believed that Moses received the Ten Commandments.

In addition to the burning bush, this desert monastery is home to an amazing collection of religious iconography, artwork, and manuscripts (some of which can be seen in the on-site museum).

The majority of tourists in this area combine a visit to St. Catherine's with a trek up Mount Sinai to see the dawn or sunset. If you want an easy route, follow the camel path; if you want better views, climb the renowned Steps of Repentance.

16. Sands of the Red Sea

Hurghada beach with umbrellas

Travelers seeking a break from touring temples might find stretches of beach along Egypt's Red Sea shoreline. The resorts dotted around the shoreline near Hurghada come to life in the winter when European families go there as part of vacation packages. The main benefit of picking a resort on the Red Sea coast over one on the Sinai Peninsula is that Luxor is readily accessible by day trip, making this the greatest location to visit for beach life while still being close to some of Egypt's most iconic landmarks.

The two major tourist towns are Hurghada and El Gouna, whereas Marsa Alam is considerably further south and is a tiny, still-developing town.

17. Egyptian Copts

One of the most significant Christian landmarks in the nation is the area of Cairo known as Coptic Cairo. This area, which was formerly the Fortress of Babylon and dates to the conquest of Egypt by the Achaemenid Empire in 525 BCE, is home to Cairo's oldest surviving church, synagogue, and mosque in addition to the excellent Coptic Museum, which houses the largest collection of Coptic Christian art and antiquities in the entire world.

The district's entrance is located on a portion of the Fortress of Babylon's walls, which were enlarged and renovated during the Roman era. Visit the Hanging Church, which has a beautiful collection of icons and was constructed partially above a water wheel from the Roman period (thus the church's name). The Holy Family with the newborn Jesus resided here in safety after escaping King Herod, according to local legend, before making their way down the small alley to the Church of St. Sergius and Bacchus.

The Ben Ezra Synagogue nearby is well-known for being the location where the Geniza document trove was found. The Amr Ibn Al-As Mosque, which was constructed by the Arab Muslim army commander (and subsequently the first governor of Egypt) after conquering Egypt, is only a short walk away.

18. Al-Hitan Wadi

In the Fayoum region, a beautiful and fertile depression fed by antiquated canals and bordered by desert lies Wadi Al-Hitan. Although the Fayoum itself is a fascinating spot to explore, with Lake Quran, Tunis, a pottery town, and scattered Pharaonic monuments across the hinterland, the major draw here is the UNESCO World Heritage site of Wadi Al-Hitan in the surrounding desert.

The discovery of a gigantic fossil hoard of the basilosaurus and dorodontus, two of the earliest ancient whales, among the valley's orange dunes and rough rocks greatly aided human knowledge of whale development.

Walking paths leading from the tourist center out to skeletal sites buried in the sand are some of the findings that have been left in their original locations.
Wadi Al-significance Hitan's is well explained at the museum located in the tourist center, which also showcases many of the other discoveries made there, including an 18-meter-long basilosaurus whale skeleton.

19. Hostel of Hathor

Although Dendara itself was a significant religious site from the beginning of Ancient Egypt, the Temple of Hathor at Dendera was constructed in the late Pharaonic era and expanded throughout the Roman era.
Due to the temple's youth (in comparison to other Pharaonic temples), it is one of the

most complete remaining temples in Egypt, making a journey here well worth a day trip from Luxor.

Here, the reliefs and decorations are well maintained. The columns topped with the heads of the Egyptian goddess Hathor and the wall reliefs of the Roman Emperor Tiberius paying homage to the Egyptian gods should be particularly noted when in the hypostyle hall, which was constructed by Tiberius. Dendera is located 80 kilometers north of Luxor, just outside the city of Qena.

20. Church of St. Anthony

The Monastery of St. Anthony has been a functioning monastery since the fourth century and is continuously inhabited by around 120 monks today. It is hidden amid the rough northern highlands of the Red Sea coast. Within the fortress-like enclosure, the Church of St. Anthony includes secco wall paintings that date from the 11th and 12th centuries and are regarded as one of the most significant collections of Egyptian Coptic art in the world. The church, which is a popular site for Egyptian Coptic Christians on their annual pilgrimage, also houses the burial of St. Anthony, the founder of monasticism.

Monks provide tours of the monastery that enable visitors to see the church, and portions of the gardens, and even climb up and stroll on top of the walls. The monastery at St. Anthony's is extremely far away. Hiring a driver from Cairo or Hurghada is the most convenient way to get here if you don't have your transportation.

EGYPT'S BEST TRADITIONAL FOOD AND RESTAURANTS

TEN OF EGYPT'S BEST TRADITIONAL FOOD

Egypt's cuisine, which has a history as old as its ancient monuments, mainly depends on the vast wealth of fruits and vegetables that are annually collected in the lush Nile Delta. Since it is difficult and expensive to raise cattle in Egypt, many traditional meals are vegetarian now, however, most recipes may be modified to include meat. Offal, beef, lamb, and other meats are often utilized, while seafood is popular along the shore. Pork is not a common ingredient in traditional cuisine since the bulk of the population is Muslim. Aish Baladi, or Egyptian flatbread, fava beans, and a plethora of unique spices are staple foods.

Ful Medames

Ful medames, a straightforward meal of stewed fava beans, is a traditional Egyptian cuisine. The first evidence of fava beans being consumed by humans comes from a Neolithic site close to Nazareth, Israel, and it's believed that the meal originated in Egypt during the pharaonic period. Nowadays, ful medames, or ful as it is more often called, is served all day long but is particularly well-liked in the morning. It is available for purchase in many restaurants as a classic mezze or on the streets. In a big pot, the beans are cooked for the whole night before being spiced and seasoned with olive oil. Typically, ful medames are served with pickled vegetables and aish Baladi.

Ta'meya

Ta'meya, another wildly famous street snack, is felafel's equivalent in Egypt. Ta'meya, on the other hand, is prepared with crushed fava beans rather than chickpeas like their Middle Eastern counterparts. Typically, chopped onions, parsley, coriander, cumin, and fresh dill are added to the bean paste before it is formed into a ball and cooked. Before being fried, ta'miya are often dusted with sesame seeds to give them an additional crunch. Whether you eat them as a snack later in the day or for breakfast as most Egyptians do, they are vegan, affordable, and completely wonderful. Ta'miya is often served with a side of ful in addition to tahini sauce, salad, and aish baladi.

Mulukhiya

Egyptian staple mulukhiyah is spelled differently depending on the restaurant (variations include molokhia, molokhia, and moroheiya). It is named after the plant of the same-named plant. The green leafy vegetable mulukhiyah, sometimes known as jute in English, is nearly never offered uncooked. Instead, the leaves are coarsely chopped and stewed until they resemble a thick stew with garlic, lemon juice, and spices. The stewed leaves' texture is a little slimy due to their natural viscosity, but their taste is rich, fragrant, and a little bitter. You may serve mulukhiyah alone over rice, bread, or with pieces of meat (typically beef, chicken, or rabbit). At the seashore, seafood is a preferred addition.

Fattah

The Egyptian variant of fattah, which is well-known across the Middle East, is often connected with festivities and religious occasions. A new baby's birth and Eid al-Adha, the sacrifice feast that celebrates the end of Ramadan, are two occasions when it is offered in special. It is made up of layers of rice and fried aish baladi, with pieces of meat placed between the layers and vinegar and tomato sauce on top. Although the kind of meat used varies depending on the dish, it is often either beef, veal, or lamb, with lamb being the most traditional. Outside of the times of religious festivals, you should be able to locate fattah. But watch your calories—this meal is notoriously calorie-dense!

Kushari

Kushari is a cheap and distinctively Egyptian meal that has grown to the point that whole restaurants in Cairo and other cities are devoted to serving it alone. It is made out of rice, spaghetti, round macaroni, and black lentils, and is topped with a spicy, thick tomato sauce. Then, whole chickpeas and crispy fried onions are added as garnishes to this real jumble of ingredients. Kushari offers a unique fusion of tastes and textures that both residents and visitors find to be addicting, despite how weird this meal may seem. Also, it's vegetarian (and indeed vegan, as long as vegetable oil is used to fry the onions instead of butter)

Hamam Mashi

Although juvenile pigeon, often known as squab, is not a common meat in Western culture, it is considered a delicacy in Egypt. In dovecotes all around the country, pigeons are kept exclusively for human consumption, producing black meat with a distinctive taste. Due in part to its reputation as a delicacy and in part to its reputation as an aphrodisiac, hamam mahshi is a common option for wedding feasts. Freekeh, a cracked green wheat with a nutty taste, chopped onions, giblets, and spices are placed into a whole squab to form the meal. The chicken is then barbecued over a wood fire or roasted on a spit until its skin is crispy and golden brown.

Hawawshi

Hawawshi is a common pick-up-and-go street meal and a side dish in restaurants, but it's arguably best recognized as a component of comforting Egyptian home cuisine. It's Egypt's version of a filled meat sandwich. It is prepared in a traditional wood oven with seasoned ground beef or lamb cooked throughout the whole pocket of aish baladi bread. The bread is practically cooked when it is finished since it is so crisp. The meat combination may sometimes include chopped onion, bell pepper, or tomato in addition to other spices depending on the recipe. Try hawawshi prepared with crushed chili peppers for an added spice.

Sandwiches with liver

Many Egyptian cuisines often use liver as an ingredient. Liver sandwiches are a particular specialty in the ancient port city of Alexandria, where customers come from all around to purchase them from fast food restaurants or street sellers. Chopped calf liver is often stir-fried to perfection with garlic, bell peppers, lime, or lemon. Although important, spices differ from chef to cook. Any Alexandrian liver recipe worth its salt should have a generous amount of chile in addition to cumin, cinnamon, ginger, cloves, and/or cardamom. The cooked liver is served with pickled veggies inside a fresh Egyptian baguette or bread roll (known locally as torshi).

Sayadeya

Sayadeya is another coastal delicacy for seafood enthusiasts and is best enjoyed in seaside towns like Alexandria, Suez, and Port Said where the catch is always assured to be fresh. It makes use of white fish filets that have been gently fried after being marinated in spices and lemon juice (often bass, bluefish, or mullet). The filets are then roasted in an earthenware pot over a bed of yellow rice with a rich tomato and onion sauce on top (similar to a Moroccan tagine). The outcome? The fish is very tender and aromatic, melting at the touch of a fork.

Sayadeya often has fried onions or flakes of chili as a garnish.

Kunafa

Dessert is a must-have item on any list of foods to try, and kunafa is among Egypt's most well-liked desserts. The original form consists of two layers of very thin semolina flour noodles, which are traditionally offered during Ramadan to keep people satisfied during the hours of fasting. These are constructed around a soft cheese filling (often ricotta) in the center and cooked until crisp. The noodles may also be swapped out for thin strips of filo pastry or spun shredded wheat, while the filling options range from custard to mixed nuts. Some Egyptian bakers are becoming more creative with their kunafa fillings; current versions include mango, chocolate, and even avocado.

The Top 10 Cairo Restaurants for Locals and Visitors

1. 1901's Le Pacha

Best restaurants in Cairo, Egypt: Le Pacha 1901

Place: Zamalek

Dress code: sophisticated casual

Price per person: 300–800 EGP

Yes, alcohol is served.

In the Nile, yes

There are vegan and vegetarian alternatives available.

Le Pacha, which has won several international awards, is at the top of the list because it technically has multiple excellent restaurants on a single Nile-docked boat rather than just one or two.

Le Pacha has 7 distinct dining options and one bar/lounge/nightclub-like establishment. Our top picks include Carlo's, where you can order shisha and choose from a variety of international cuisines; L'Asiatique, their pan-Asian restaurant, which was named the third best in Africa; and Piccolo Mondo, an Italian restaurant with a view of the Nile.

We'll be the first to inform you that their cuisine is consistently excellent. And while it may seem obvious, it's not in Egypt. It's awful when you can tell when a change chef is in charge at a restaurant since consistency is usually a problem, but Le Pacha's locations consistently deliver. Single. Time. Other eateries include Le Steak (French), Le Tarbouche (Egyptian), River Boat

(Lebanese), Maharani (Indian), and Le J.Z. (lounge).

2. Abou El Sid

Zamalek, Heliopolis, 6th of October, and New Cairo are the locations.

attire is casual.

Price per person: 300-600 EGP

Yes, alcohol is served.

Nile perspective, no

There are vegan and vegetarian alternatives available.

If you want traditional Egyptian cuisine in a very calming environment, Abou El Sid is the place to go. For more information, see our post on 12 Local Egyptian Foods You Need To Try (the decor, music, and wall art is enough to make it worth it). They also sell shisha and alcoholic drinks with Egyptian twists, such as vodka and fresh sugarcane juice. Their sharqisseya, a chicken dish with walnut sauce, packed vine leaves, Egyptian moussaka, an eggplant stew served with rice, and a medley of all their different Egyptian mezzes are among the dishes that are worth tasting. Drool.

3. Koshary Abou Tarek

Best restaurants in Cairo, Egypt: Koshary Abou Tarek

Place: Downtown

attire is casual.

Price: less than 20 EGP per individual

No alcohol was served.

Nile perspective, no

There are vegan and vegetarian choices available, and koshary is vegan by nature.
This restaurant is not at all a classy, ambiance-filled, or romantic place to eat (unless your idea of romance is very very quirky, and in that case, rock on).

In Downtown, there is a restaurant called Koshary Abou Tarek, which is recognized for serving some of the *best* koshary in the area. You may be wondering what koshary is. I'd be happy to share it with you. One of Egypt's proud national foods is koshary, which consists of rice, macaroni, lentils, chickpeas, and fried onions with a tomato sauce flavored with garlic.

It's 100% vegan, it's quick (see the guys working the koshary line, it's remarkable), it's cheap (a big dish will cost you less than 30 EGP, which is roughly $1.50), it's filling—the word "filling" is underlined seventeen times. It is not light. However, it's a fantastic power dish that will keep you going all day.

4. Pier 88

Place: Zamalek

smart-casual is OK.

Price per person: 300–1000 EGP

Yes, alcohol is served.

In the Nile, yes

There are vegan and vegetarian alternatives available.

The Red Sea resort town of El Gouna is where Pier 88 first opened as a restaurant and bar. As the cuisine and atmosphere there gained popularity, the proprietors made the bold move to expand their business to Cairo.

The Nile is visible from the top deck of the moored boat in Zamalek where Pier 88 is located. During the day, it is one of those understatedly elegant restaurants with an open kitchen and cocktails on the deck.

Reservations are advised since there is more of a nightclub vibe throughout the evening. Weekend evenings include louder music and sporadic dancing around the tables (we don't advise dining during dancing since there won't be much space to use your knife and fork).

5. Mariota, Andrea

Place: New Giza

attire is casual.

Price per person: 300–800 EGP

Yes, alcohol is served.

Nile perspective, no

Available vegan and vegetarian options: sure, but very few

Andrea Mariouteya has been owned by the same family since it was founded more than 60 years ago. Previously located on the Mariouteya canal, a branch of the Nile close to the Pyramids, this Egyptian restaurant has relocated to the New Giza plateau, where it has fantastic city views. Excellent choice if you want to dine, drink, and enjoy the scenery outside!

Although it is particularly well-known for its breakfast and brunch (their feteer is a must-try!), it is also enjoyable later in the day and in the evening when the emphasis shifts to its world-famous grills. The grilled chicken and quail are well-known across the city despite their tiny menu and restricted alternatives. Local advice: Try their handmade fries as well!

6. Zooba

Location: Heliopolis, Sheikh Zayed, Madinaty, Zamalek, Maadi, and New Cairo

attire is casual.

Price per person: 50-100 EGP

No alcohol was served.

Nile perspective, no

There are vegan and vegetarian alternatives available.

All visitors to Egypt who want a "light" introduction to Egyptian street cuisine should choose Zooba. get a taste of several local cuisines without taking the risk of eating authentic street food (aka bougie street food).

Locals like Zooba because it is a finer, more upscale version of daily staples like fuul, taameya, and koshary (see our list of all the Egyptian meals you must taste in Egypt).
Over the years, Zooba has grown to be so well-liked that in addition to opening several locations around Cairo, it has also expanded to New York City.

7. Cafe Naguib Mahfouz

The place is Khan el Khalili (Old Cairo)

attire is casual.

Price per person: 200-600 EGP

No alcohol was served.

Nile perspective, no

There are vegan and vegetarian alternatives available.

A little cafe/restaurant/shisha business named after one of Egypt's most well-known authors is located deep within the famed Khan el Khalili market (click here for our comprehensive tour). The restaurant's full name is Khan el Khalili Restaurant and Naguib Mahfouz Cafe, but for convenience's sake, locals abbreviate it to Naguib Mahfouz.

When alluding to Egypt's past, one must be particular so that people don't assume we're always talking about pharaohs and pyramids. The restaurant/cafe is a tribute to Egypt's current history. While you may be wary about dining at a restaurant near Khan el Khalili, be assured that Naguib Mahfouz Cafe is owned and operated by Oberoi Hotels and has both air conditioning and a reliable kitchen.

Their café provides shishas, a wide variety of fresh juices, and sweets, while their restaurant area serves traditional Egyptian and foreign cuisine.

8. Crimson

Place: Zamalek

Dress code: sophisticated casual

Price per person: 300–800 EGP (not including cocktails)

Yes, alcohol is served.

In the Nile, yes

There are vegan and vegetarian alternatives available.

Not much more needs to be said beyond the fact that Gloria Gaynor visited Crimson when she was in Cairo. And the likelihood is that you will experience the same emotions as the I Will Survive queen.

With both inside and outdoor patio seating, Crimson is located on the top of a Zamalek skyscraper and overlooks the Nile. The cuisine is excellent, and the view is breathtaking. They provide a wide variety of delicious appetizers, pasta, and grill specialties, plus one of Cairo's longest cocktail lists.

One of the few restaurants in Cairo that open at 8 am, they also offer breakfast and brunch, however, the food isn't as delicious in the morning as it is in the evening.

9. Pavilion 139

Address: Haram

Price per person: 300–800 EGP

Yes, alcohol is served.

Nile perspective, no

There are vegan and vegetarian alternatives available.

An oasis from the hustle and bustle of Giza is this outdoor dining area of the venerable Marriott Mena House hotel. What a prospect to have breakfast, lunch, or supper next to a fountain, surrounded by flowers, vegetation, and, of course, THE PYRAMIDS!

There is an a la carte menu as well as an all-you-can-eat buffet option. Even if the Pyramids aren't usually lit up at night, you can still see them, yet something is soothing and tranquil about the darkness.

10. Prince Kebdet

Place: Imbaba

Price varies depending on what (and how much) you purchase, but it is reasonable.

No alcohol was served.

Nile perspective, no

There are vegan and vegetarian alternatives available.

Kebdet el Prince is presently closed for transferring to a new site, as of September 2022. Kebdet el Prince, or "El Brens" as we locals call it, is a must-visit whether you're a native or a traveler who likes to dine adventurously.

The fact that this restaurant is packed shows how amazing the cuisine is even though it is neither posh nor in a popular area. like, constantly. Kebdet el Prince, which translates to "the prince of the liver," is a favorite among both regular Egyptian locals and Egyptian celebrities due to its hard-core, homestyle Egyptian menu, which is packed with traditional favorites that are difficult to find anywhere other than an Egyptian grandmother's kitchen.

The eatery is open till the wee hours of the morning, and reservations are accepted only in that order (the restaurant is rows and rows of sidewalk tables). You arrive, place your order, chow down until you're stuffed to the gills, and then clear a space for the next ravenous patron.

Although their cuisine is not for the faint of heart, it will be an unforgettable experience.

10 Arabic Phrases & Words to Improve Your Egypt Trip

With so many dialects that differ regionally and sounds that are unfamiliar to an English speaker, Arabic may be a challenging language to master. Even if Egyptian Arabic has its own peculiarities, tourists will discover that learning a few fundamental words is worth the time and effort since it's a great way to repay the legendary Egyptian hospitality you'll encounter while on your expedition. Here are some words you may use to make the most of your trip to Egypt, whether you're seeing the pharaonic kingdoms or scouring Cairo's alleys for the tastiest bowl of koshary.

As-salaam alaikum: Peace be upon you (السلام عليكم)

This is an all-purpose greeting that may be abbreviated to "salaam," which means "peace," and it is favorably appreciated almost anywhere. Even if you quickly transition to English, beginning your talk with a local welcome shows respect and friendliness. "Wa alaikum salaam," which means "peace be upon you as well," is the proper answer.

Sabah al-khair: Good morning (صباح الخير)

Cairo hums with life late into the night: locals of all ages spend hours mingling over Turkish coffee, backgammon, shisha water pipes, and selfies. Outdoor cafés seem to sprout up from the pavement as soon as the sun sets. The call to prayer reverberates through the streets immediately after the sun rises over the east bank of the Nile after each hectic night. In the early morning hours in Cairo, there is a brief period of calm before the day's heat takes hold. On your approach to breakfast, you may say "sabah al-khair," or "good morning," to your neighbor and get a groggy "sabah al-noor," or "morning light."

Shukran: Thank you (شكراً)

Everywhere you go, you should learn how to say "thank you," according to seasoned travelers, and this tiny act of courtesy is especially appreciated in Egypt. Fortunately, the phrase is simple and acceptable to say anytime you want to show thanks, regardless of whether you are purchasing a fresh mango juice or having your ticket to a tomb or temple torn. You'll almost probably get an enthusiastic "afwan" in reply, which means "you're welcome."

Lazeeza: Delicious (لذيذ)

Keep this one close by since there is only one word to describe the crunchy fava bean falafel, fresh tahini that can be poured over anything and everything, and the grilled tomatoes and eggplant that have been marinated in olive oil. The regional mainstay and authentic supper of the people, koshary, is my particular favorite food. With rice, spaghetti, lentils, and chickpeas—all topped with tomato sauce and fried onions—it is the epitome of comfort cuisine. Just before serving, you should drizzle an unique vinegar and garlic dressing over everything to truly elevate the meal. Lazeeza, for sure.

Najma: Stars (نجوم)

I was aware to watch out for intricate hieroglyphics, crisp lines, and proportioned things before I went to Egypt. I was aware that the ancient Egyptians portrayed creatures, humans, deities, and landscapes using vivid colors and their own dynasty aesthetic. Even the well-known locations offered surprises, and seeing these masterpieces in reality was as magnificent as advertised. I wasn't expecting the star-painted ceilings that were present in every tomb and temple. More than any other aspect, this one brought me closer to the ancients and offered as a concrete reminder that they likely had the same feeling of amazement that we do while stargazing today when they peered up at the night sky above the Nile.

Jameela: Beautiful (جميل)

Egypt's famous river, the Nile, covers the whole length of the country, and sailing it is still one of the greatest ways to observe the everyday rhythms of local life. From a ship, you can see how lush marshes give way to productive farming and neat rows of date palms. The gorgeous landscape, which is every shade of green, is rendered even more stunning by the ominous brown desert in the background. A child beside the river pulls a flopping fish with a handmade rod as a flock of snow-white egrets take off suddenly from the reeds. You can see why people are drawn to the river valley when you consider how little this site has altered over the many millennia since humans first inhabited it. Beyond the fact that it sustains life, it is wholly jameela.

Ma'an: Water (مَيِـه)

The Nile was revered by the ancient Egyptians, and it now provides for close to 100 million Egyptians as well as many others in East Africa. The vast river and its essential ma'an continue to be the core of Egyptian life. Families celebrate birthdays, couples of all ages promenade, and young men swim to escape the oppressive heat on Cairo's expansive riverbank walkways. Many of the same operations can be seen in Upper Egypt, where the agricultural sector also dominates and is dependent on river irrigation. Although the river doesn't flood anymore, the water is still useful.

Habibi: My love (حبيبي)

The price was rising quickly and I couldn't get her attention until, in a move I could only get away with as a foreign man, I dropped "habibi," a term of endearment commonly used for all kinds of sweet talking. I was in a dusty spice shop in Aswan trying to smell my way through the list of seasonings I wanted to take home, and the fast-talking spice dealer was adding items to my bag faster than I could say "shukran." It's common in Egyptian pop music, and mothers use it with their children and close friends. The seller in my situation offered me a better price for my spices and included a complimentary bag of sweets. She also said she had misjudged me.

Insha Allah: God willing (إن شاء الله)

Will we have excellent weather tomorrow? is a common inquiry that is answered in Egypt with this phrase rather than a simple "yes" or "no." Allah willing. Will the ship set sail on schedule? Allah willing. On the surface, the phrase suggests that nothing happens that isn't God's will, but in practice it allows the user to express their hopes that something might happen, while conveniently abdicating responsibility for any specific outcome. Even a goodbye as innocent as "see you tomorrow" is answered with "insha Allah." Once you get used to hearing it, you may grow to value the informal admonition to be flexible and anticipate the unexpected in Egypt.

Yalla: Let's go (يلا)

The high point of many tourists' trips to Egypt is their Egyptologist guide. Each new monument is contextualized and explained with competence, compassion, and critical thinking around what these places signify for Egyptians and for the rest of the globe while you are exploring with one of these specialists. Each morning began with a summary of what I would see, followed by a wave and a brief "yalla"—"let's go"—from my guide. As I learned more about the country throughout my travels, I didn't need as much explanation to place the sites in history. I want you to start thinking about the word immediately as the joyful anticipation of new experiences. Yalla!

Conclusion

And, that's a wrap for this comprehensive Egypt guide book with itineraries! I hope that it's served as a trip planner and a useful guide for you on what to expect when traveling in Egypt!

Printed in Great Britain
by Amazon

15623945R00119